FRENCH PRINTS OF THE 20TH CENTURY

FRENCH PRINTS
OF THE 20TH CENTURY

Roger Passeron

PALL MALL PRESS · LONDON

Translated from the French
by Robert Allen

Pall Mall Press Ltd.
5 Cromwell Place, London S.W. 7

First published in Great Britain in 1970

© 1970 by Office du Livre, Fribourg
Reproduction rights reserved by SPADEM, Paris
and COSMOPRESS, Geneva
All rights reserved

SBN 269 02655 x

Printed in Switzerland

Contents

Introduction

Engraving is the art of the engraver. It is also the act by which an artist expresses his thought, his testimony, his sensibility, his poetry, his message. Thirdly, it is the tangible product of this act, the print produced by the printer's press to convey the aesthetic emotion that the artist had felt in the act of creation. What beauty, what feeling, what joy there is in a fine engraving! What a source of inexhaustible wonder it is for the happy art lover who discovers the universe it holds! What never-ending delights it offers! And the pleasure it gives us never loses its intensity and is always there for us to recover at sad times and gay, whenever we look at it, love it, reflect upon it, bring it to life. . . .

"Engraving is infinity. . . ." André Masson said. Every single day, for close on six centuries, artists have produced engravings. And no two of them are alike, just as the engraving of today is unlike that of tomorrow. Engraving is an endless renas-cence, and the artist can use it in endless different ways.

"It is almost unbelievable," Dunoyer de Segonzac once told me, "that one can, by means of a small rectangle of metal, stone or wood, capture so much sky and space, render the poetry of nature, convey to others the impressions, deep or superficial, which one feels, and all that so intensely, with such communicative force, even at a distance of centuries."

"Even if only a single proof were pulled from each plate," Picasso has said, "I should still be strongly attached to this mode of expression because it enables me to express myself completely."

This book is an anthology of engravings by the greatest artists who, in France, have been deeply interested in that mode of expression and in the twentieth century have given it the important place that it deserves. Hence the reader must not be

7

surprised to find that the same eulogistic epithets recur again and again in the descriptions of the various works. For each artist the author has sought out either his masterpiece or the most significant of his prints. And it is necessary to make this clear in each description in order to place the works in their proper perspective. I trust the reader will understand this and will forgive the repetition of adjectives which, besides expressing the author's enthusiasm, betoken the exceptional quality of the prints he has selected. Unfortunately his selection cannot embrace all the works of capital importance, for this century, though its end is hardly yet in sight, is far too rich in engravings for that.

According to Jean Adhémar, Chief Curator of the Print Room in the French National Library, the twentieth century began in 1890 as far as engraving was concerned. Therefore, if we want to follow the complex development of the various movements it comprises, we must find out what influences the generation of 1890 was exposed to. It has even been said that twentieth-century engraving began as early as 1864, the year Edouard Manet did his lithograph *The Races*. Although the author of this book does not want to go back quite so far, he has started with an engraving of 1896 because it foreshadows the freedom of handling that characterizes those of the present day. For the same reason it is followed by others, all done between 1894 and 1899, by such important artists as Gauguin, Signac, Munch, Toulouse-Lautrec, Bonnard and Vuillard. If these men are the fathers of twentieth-century engraving, the works they produced must perforce be given a place in our century because many artists who followed in their footsteps viewed them as their masters and found inspiration in their example; whereas some artists who were born in the nineteenth century and died in the twentieth have their rightful place in a work

devoted to nineteenth-century engraving. On the other hand, many painter-engravers who have come to the fore since 1950 are not included in this book because a certain distance is needed to form a definitive opinion of their works and recognize those of capital importance, which too few exhibitions or the lack of special studies prevent our being acquainted with. It may be recalled in this connection that Picasso's *The Frugal Meal*, though engraved in 1904, was hardly known at all before 1945.

Lastly, and more important still, this book is too small to include all the artists who deserve a place in it. Obviously it lays no claim to be all-embracing. The author has had to make an extremely stringent selection and is well aware that there is room for a different work, devoted, for instance, to the engravings produced during the last twenty years by other artists, so rich and promising are the schools of young engravers at the present time. Such a book would, however, be informed by a different spirit from this one, which is made up of masterpieces. Since we lack the distance needed for establishing a hierarchy of values, a book on more recent engravings could only present a haphazard sample. It would undoubtedly be interesting, but would have a different character from the anthology selected for the present work.

Before giving a few brief definitions that may help the enquiring reader to understand how engravings are made, I think it is advisable to point out, after the general definition, why they are made and to emphasize the difference between an original engraving and a reproduction, which has neither authenticity nor artistic value.

An engraving is first of all a drawing. It is a drawing done by an artist on a flat surface that is harder than paper. This surface may be wood (for a woodcut), soft stone (for a lithograph) metal, (e.g. copper, for a drypoint, line engraving or etching) or some other substance.

This drawing on a relatively hard surface may be done with steel tools—a gouge for wood, a needle or burin for metal—or with special crayons or brushes for lithographic stone.

The finished drawing is inked with special printing ink. A sheet of slightly dampened paper is applied to the surface thus prepared and the two are run together through a hand press. This is done by a pressman for wood, a copperplate printer for metal, a lithographic printer for stone. The ink must be transferred entirely from the drawing to the paper, if the artist's idea is not to be falsified. The paper is now called a proof, a plate, a print : the general term is an engraving.

An engraving is more than just a drawing. That is why engravings are made. In fact, the incised and inked line is far finer, livelier, more intense, more radiant. In an engraving the heavy lines are more forceful and violent; the thin ones subtler and more agile. The blacks are matchless for their beauty, depth and velvety intensity; the grays for their delicate gradations. All these qualities are exclusive to original engravings and make it easy to distinguish them, when in good condition, from even the best reproductions. The latter, in fact, are not genuine; they do not radiate; they lack the life which the artist gives the engravings he does himself and which cannot be replaced by any photo-mechanical process, however perfect. It takes the artist's own hand to create an engraving; without that hand even the most elaborate process produces merely a semblance without a soul.

I must, however, emphasize that one does not have to be a bigoted purist and, for love of the pure engraver's unique skill, take offense on seeing some great painter make use of bases obtained with mechanical methods. When a painter-engraver resorts to a base of this type—Dali and Rouault have employed heliogravure, Picasso utilized photolithography for his *Italian Girl*—and uses it to produce a personal work by re-working the stone or metal plate himself, we must consider the final result as an original engraving. It would be wrong to pronounce a dogmatic anathema that would deprive us of major works by Rouault, Dali, Picasso, Braque and Chagall—to mention only artists represented in this book—who occasionally made use of a surface on which a design was already reproduced by a photo-mechanical process but who subsequently engraved that surface themselves.

Lastly, let me state my preference for engravings made by painters, which are so rich in warmth and sensuality and far excel the works of pure engravers, however amazing their technical virtuosity may be. I would recall, in this context, that it took Dunoyer de Segonzac, one of the greatest engravers of our century, only one twenty-minute lesson to learn engraving.

Although, in the next chapter, an attempt is made to answer the question so often asked : "How is an engraving made ?" it should be remembered that the pleasure and excitement a print gives us do not depend in the slightest on a knowledge of the technique that the artist employed.

The principal engraving techniques

The many different techniques used in print making have one thing in common—the paper. It is the paper that provides the "white" in a print. It is the paper that gives the light. This is so true that when different papers—antique, rice, Japanese vellum, Rives—are employed for printing a given plate the result is, at least in the eyes of a connoisseur, the same number of different prints. Consequently, artists choose their paper with the utmost care, particularly for the first three or four pulls which, for this reason, are called "trial prints" and are, as a rule, marked as such by the artist when he signs them.

Here the reader will find descriptions of ten engraving techniques. This will put him in a position to form a better idea of how the prints presented in this book were produced. They are the techniques most commonly used at the present time. Each artist chooses those best suited to his tem-

perament and inspiration. Needless to say, he is perfectly free to employ more than one technique in a given print. In fact, some artists have made much use of this privilege, inventing variants and even, like Picasso, creating new methods for their engraving.

The descriptions of these processes apply equally well to prints in black and white and to prints in color. It must be borne in mind, however, that the latter may be produced either with a single plate or block inked in a different color before each impression—this was the method used by Derain for the print reproduced here—or, more commonly, by using a different one for each color, as was done for all the other prints in this book. Each plate or block is registered by means of two holes and two pins that are made to coincide at each impression in order to prevent the colors from overlapping unless the artist so desires.

Lorjou : *The Cat*, woodcut. *(The Bestiary.)*
Editions d'Auteuil.
Private Collection.

WOODCUT
One of the oldest methods of engraving (early fifteenth century)

End wood: The block is cut against the grain of the wood, like a slice of a tree trunk. The grain does not show in the finished print.

Side wood: The block is cut along the grain, like a board used in carpentry. The grain shows up in the finished print.

The artist draws the design directly on the block with a pen or pencil, or sketches it with a paintbrush. Then with a steel tool—a knife or gouge—he reserves the design by cutting away the wood parallel to the lines, which are left intact. As a result the design appears in relief on the woodblock. The block is inked and a sheet of paper laid over it. The two are run through the press by a master printer and the proof thus produced is commonly called a woodcut.

LITHOGRAPHY
Discovered by Senefelder and Schmid about 1796

A fine-grained flat surface is prepared on a block of limestone.

The artist draws the design on this surface with a greasy crayon. The crayon line is held by the grain of the stone. As far as the artist is concerned, there is no practical difference between this procedure and drawing on paper. When the design is finished a lithograph printer takes the stone and fixes the design with an acid in a very watery solution. The fixed grease of the design repels the water, which is absorbed instead by the rest of the stone. When the stone is inked with a roller the design holds the ink, which the damp areas do not. Now it only necessary to apply a sheet of paper to the stone and run both through a press together. The paper is carefully stripped from the stone, giving what is called a lithographic print.

Instead of a greasy crayon, the artist may use a pen or paintbrush dipped in special lithographic ink. The stone must be very thick to prevent breakage; this makes it heavy and cumbersome. As a result, since the last century artists have used transfer paper. This permits the design to be transferred with ease to the lithographic stone. However, the blacks obtained by drawing directly on the stone are always finer, intenser and more velvety than those produced with transfer paper.

The lithograph reproduced here is a likeness of Picasso's children. He did it with his fingers dipped in the ink, which he diluted more or less in order to obtain the shades of gray he wanted. Using crayons or lithographic ink the same results can be obtained with a zinc plate as with a stone. The print produced in this way is called a "zinc lithograph."

Trémois: *The Art of Love*, line engraving.
Published by Club du Livre, 1962.
Private Collection.

Picasso: *Paloma and Claude*, lithograph, trial print.
Private Collection.

LINE ENGRAVING
The oldest method of engraving on metal; fifteenth century

The tool used for line engraving is called a burin. It is a small steel blade, triangular or lozenge-shaped in cross section, ground at a slant and with the blunt end set in a mushroom-shaped wooden handle that the engraver holds in the hollow of his hand. He grasps and guides the point between thumb and forefinger and pushes it, always in the same direction, in order to cut a furrow in the uncoated, polished copperplate. He holds the plate in the other hand and turns it to suit the direction he wants to give the line. Line engraving is a cold and difficult art, and it takes a resolute character to incise a design in clean lines with no corrections.

The furrows or lines cut in the copperplate are inked. The surface of the plate is wiped so that the ink is left only in the hollows that form the design. The plate is laid on a sheet of dampened paper, and both are run through a copperplate printing press together. On peeling the paper from the plate one finds that all the ink, in other words the design, has been transferred to the paper. A proof obtained in this way is commonly called a line engraving.

Picasso: *Minotaur Caressing a Sleeping Girl*, drypoint. Published first by Vollard, later by Petiet. Private Collection.

DRYPOINT
Late fifteenth century

The artist draws on the uncoated, polished copperplate with a point in the same way as he would with a pencil on a sheet of paper. The point may be either a steel needle or a diamond chip set in a handle. The point cuts a hollow line and at the same time raises a minute ridge of copper in relief, called a "burr." These burrs hold the ink and give the line in a drypoint a peculiar velvety quality. Inking and proofing are done as for line engraving.

Since copper is a soft metal the burrs soon become flattened under the press. For this reason a drypoint engraving can only be produced in a small number of prints if uniform quality is to be maintained.

The number of proofs pulled can be increased (as in the case of the engraving reproduced here) by depositing galvanoplastically a thin layer (2 to 5 microns) of iron over the whole surface of the copperplate after the trial proofs have been pulled. This process is called steel plating, though the term is inaccurate because it is not steel but pure electrolytic iron that is deposited on the copper.

ETCHING
Believed to have been first used by Dürer in 1515

The polished copperplate is coated with a varnish that dries in contact with the air. The artist uses a steel point that looks like a pencil to draw on this varnish, laying bare the copper. When the design is complete the plate is immersed in an acid bath, usually nitric acid or iron perchloride. This causes

14

a chemical corrosion that deepens the lines of the design. The process is called biting. Needless to say, only the parts laid bare by the point are bitten for the varnish protects the other areas. Thus the action of the bath does not add any lines to the artist's original drawing. It merely deepens the design to a greater or lesser extent as the artist himself decides, depending on whether the biting is more or less prolonged. The varnish is then removed with a solvent. Inking and printing are done as in the preceding techniques.

In an etching the point glides over the copperplate without incising the metal. This allows the engraver the utmost freedom and renders every turn and twist. Zinc, nickel or steel may be used instead of copper, and the point may be replaced with a sewing needle (as in Segonzac's *Ronsard*). The acid may be strong or weak, ranging from nitric acid with 10 per cent of water (very strong) as used by André Masson to the very soft acid used by Segonzac, 8–10 degrees Baumé. The biting process may last as little as one minute or as long as several hours : that is a matter for the artist to decide for himself to suit his temperament and sensibility.

Dunoyer de Segonzac : *Fernande with Clasped Hands*, etching.
Published by Petiet.
Private Collection.

SOFT-GROUND ETCHING
Soft-ground etching was particularly popular in the eighteenth century

The polished copperplate is coated with a varnish that remains soft. A sheet of grained paper is laid over it. The artist draws on this paper with a pencil in the usual way, so that the lines of the design adhere to the varnish. When the paper is removed, the copper is bared solely where the pencil left its mark. The plate is bitten with an acid as in an etching of the usual type. Then the varnish is dissolved and the plate is inked and printed as described above for other copper engraving techniques.

Valadon : *Women Drying Themselves*, soft-ground etching.
Private Collection.

AQUATINT
A process for engraving on copper that dates from
the seventeenth century

The polished copperplate is sprinkled with grains
of resin that may be more or less minute. It is then
heated to melt the grains until they coalesce and
stick to the plate, but without melting completely.

This leaves interstices between them. During the
biting process the acid penetrates to the copper
only through these interstices.

As a result, when the resin is removed the surface
of the copper presents a grain or roughness that
holds the ink and produces the effect of a wash
drawing (as in Goya's prints). The artist may
engrave the entire surface of the plate and make his
design appear by removing the roughness with a
tool, either a burnisher or a rounded point, as in
this print by Picasso. Or he may reserve parts of it
with a compact varnish and apply the aquatint
process only on the areas he chooses. Depending
on the size of the grains and their regular or irreg-
ular distribution over the plate, different effects are
obtained, ranging from the palest grays to the
deepest blacks, strewn with a myriad of minute
white dots. The artist may also apply other techniques over the aquatint, such as line engraving,
soft-ground or classic etching, or drypoint.

Picasso : *Musketeer Pursuing a Naked Woman*, aquatint.
Published by Galerie Louise Leiris, Paris.
Collection Louise Leiris.

Picasso : *Portrait of Vollard II*, sugar process.
Published first by Vollard, later by M. Lecomte.
Private Collection.

THE SUGAR PROCESS
A technique discovered about the middle of the nineteenth century

On the bare copperplate, either smooth or finely grained, the artist draws his design with a brush or pen loaded with Indian ink diluted with a saturated solution of sugar.

When the design is finished he leaves it to dry and then grounds the whole surface of the plate with a varnish. Once this is perfectly dry, the plate is immersed in water. The sugar of the design melts, leaving the copper bare where the pen or brush made its mark whereas the remaining areas are protected by the varnish. The copper is bitten with acid. This process may be used by a draughtsman to draw his design with pen and ink or by a painter to do a wash drawing directly onto the plate.

MEZZOTINT
Technique invented by Ludwig von Siegen in the seventeenth century

This technique involves the overall abrasion of the copperplate with a tool called a cradle. The process makes the surface of the plate resemble a piece of velvet in which every tiny hair is replaced by a copper point. After preparing the plate in this way the artist draws the design using, instead of a pencil, a tool that may be a rounded point, a burnisher or a scraper which crushes the copper points. With the plate inked and the print pulled, the lines drawn on the copper appear in white or in various shades of gray, depending on their strength, namely on whether they have polished the copper to a greater or lesser degree so that it holds more or less ink. The rest of the print is a rich, velvety black. The cradle is a flat steel blade, grooved and set in a handle. It is held perpendicular to the surface of the plate and rocked to and fro —hence the name cradle—advancing a minute fraction of an inch at each stroke. This tool is like

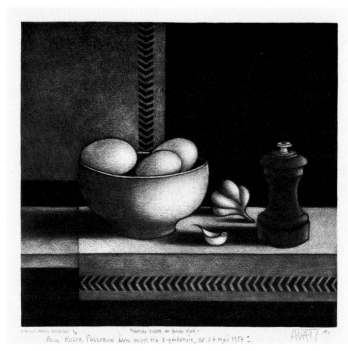

Avati: *Still Life with Garlic*, mezzotint.
Private Collection.

a hand, each groove representing a finger; but a hand with 70–100 fingers, each of which digs a tiny cavity in the plate. Thus 70–100 cavities are made at each stroke. When the process is finished a copperplate measuring 30 × 20 cm. has certainly more than a million such cavities. That is what gives the velvety effect. In order to obtain an absolutely black print there must be at least 2500 cavities every square inch.

LINOCUT
Engraving on linoleum—early twentieth century

This technique is identical to the woodcut. To make a colored linocut the artist can choose one of three methods. He may use a single piece of linoleum and apply different colors to the different parts of the design. He may use a number of engraved plates equal to the number of colors he wants and print them, adequately registered, one after the other. This is the method employed by Picasso in the print reproduced here, which required six plates for the six colors. The third method is that used by Picasso in his more recent linocuts. It consists in taking a single piece of linoleum and engraving it alongside the printing press. First the uncut plate is inked with a given color and run through the press; this produces a plain ground color on the paper. Then Picasso takes the plate in hand and cuts a design with a gouge or other tool. He selects another color and the plate is printed on the previously obtained ground. He repeats the process as many times as he likes. This method involves printing the successive states of the print one over the other. Unlike all the other techniques described in this book, it does not permit of producing additional complete prints with what is left of the linoleum. Consequently, the entire edition must be printed at each state. It is obvious too that the artist must start out with the palest colors. Picasso has shown great interest in this process and so far he is the only artist who has succeeded in producing master works with it.

It often happens that after pulling the first few proofs an artist feels the need to make some alterations. In this case he works over his plate and pulls additional proofs. The first are called proofs of the first state; the second proofs of the second state, and so on. Picasso has gone as far as thirty-one states. Segonzac, instead, makes do as a rule with a single state.

Picasso : *Bust of a Girl after the Younger Cranach*, linocut.
Published by Galerie Louise Leiris.
Collection Louise Leiris.

When the artist has finished working on his plate, he has a few "trial prints" pulled, chooses the one he considers closest to his inspiration, and marks it "Press Proof : prints on such and such a paper." This press proof serves as a model for the printer who, as a skilled master of his trade, pulls the required number of prints identical with the model and takes pride in doing the job so precisely that one print is indistinguishable from the rest.

Then, as a rule, the artist has his plate scored in order to make sure that no further prints can be pulled from it against his will. This is not done for commercial reasons but because he must be able to check the quality of the impression and make sure that he has not been traduced. For the same reason it is customary for the artist to sign each print; the first to do this was Seymour Haden in the mid-nineteenth century. During the second third of that century it also became the custom to number each print in sequence with a fraction. The denominator represents the total number of prints made from the plate, the numerator that of the order of printing. As a rule the artist reserves a few proofs —from five to fifteen—for his own use, authenticating them with the indication "artist's proof," either with or without a serial number.

These rules are not absolute. There are many examples of prints, some of them masterpieces, that were neither signed nor authenticated by the artist. On the other hand, I know of mechanical reproductions—for instance, photolithographs of oil paintings or watercolors—which, though not original engravings, were signed and even numbered by the artist.

I have done my best to keep these technical explanations as concise as possible. I hope, nonetheless, that they will help the reader to appreciate to the full the work of the engraver. But what really counts is for the artist to communicate to the spectator by means of an authentic work of art the emotion he felt in the creative act, and it matters little what medium he has chosen if he fails to do that.

The artists

This lithograph in eight colors is undoubtedly the finest of all Renoir's prints.

In my opinion it is far superior to those huge, confused lithographs entitled *Children Playing Ball* (or *Looking for Potatoes*, an alternative title) and *The Pinned Hat*. Indeed it was the success met with by this *Standing Bather* that led Ambroise Vollard to commission those two prints.

Renoir was no great draughtsman. For that reason he produced few prints—fifty-five in all, of which thirty-one are lithographs and twenty-four etchings and soft-grounds. But the plate I have selected is very fine indeed and has great qualities. Its warm, vaporous highlights led Claude Roger-Marx to say that it was as youthful as a Watteau and as sensual as a Fragonard.

It was made in the workshop of that master lithographic printer, Auguste Clot, whose collaboration enabled such great painter-engravers as Degas, Bonnard, Vuillard, Toulouse-Lautrec, Munch, Signac and Redon to produce lithographic masterpieces in both color and black and white.

Renoir did the original drawing on transfer paper, after which it was transferred by Clot to eight lithographic stones—one for each color. The softness and delicacy of the tints are amazing. I know of no other color lithograph by a great master in which the colors have such subtle lightness and delicacy—and I have not forgotten Redon's *Beatrice*. When this *Standing Bather* was less well known it was often taken at first glance for a pastel. In this respect it is one of the masterpieces of color lithography. Both the composition and the handling are typical of Renoir.

The female nude was one of Renoir's favorite themes throughout his life. François Daulte has tellingly described how well "he succeeded in bringing home to us the indefinable radiance of a woman's body in full flower, how well he observed the shape of a profile half candid, half greedy, the simplicity of an artless gesture, the modeling of a hand, the long tresses that tumble over a girl's shoulder with unstudied grace."

The posture and the silhouette of this bather were inspired by Gabrielle, Renoir's pretty servant girl who was also one of his best models—she had a skin that did not repel light, as he was fond of saying. They express with amazing intimacy the modest comportment of a young woman who shields her nakedness after the bath.

This work has become very rare. When it appeared in 1896—a few early proofs were pulled both in black and white and in colors and one hundred copies produced—it was not a success. Needless to say, the stones were erased after the prints had been made.

Standing Bather, 1896.
Lithograph in eight colors, 41 × 34.5 cm.
Bibliography: L. Delteil, pl. 28; C. Roger-Marx, pl. 3.
Private Collection.

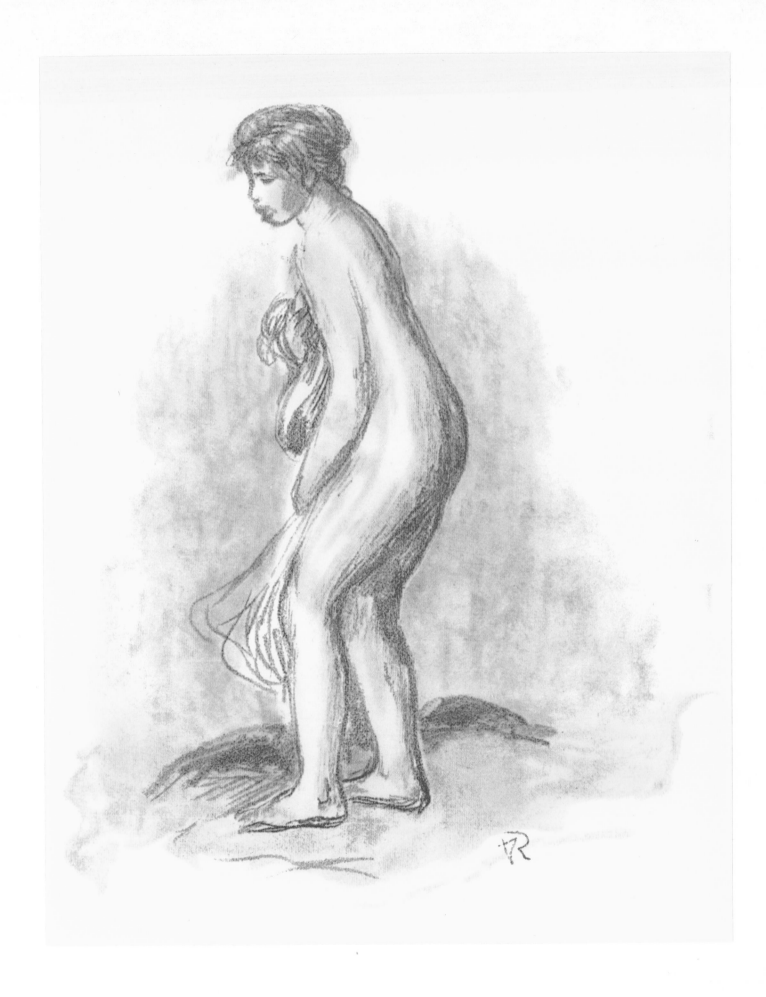

23

"I am certain that my engravings on wood, so different from anything that other artists do, will be valued some day."

Gauguin's opinion of his woodcuts is now universally accepted, but it was not until many years after his death that their value was generally recognized. When Gauguin returned, in August 1893, from his first two-year stay in Tahiti he was impatient to reveal his new vision to Parisian art circles. He had been dreadfully disappointed by the social climate of the colony but contact with the native population and "enjoyment of their free, animal and human life" had changed his views entirely. He had gone to the South Sea islands for the purpose of learning anew "to think freely," and there is no doubt that this return to the primitive sources made a very strong, definitive impact on the art of a man who said that "truth is pure intellectual art, truth is primitive art. The most scholarly of all is Egypt. . . . The great mistake is Greek, no matter how fine it may be."

In Tahiti Gauguin had done sculptures on wood. Wood carving and wood engraving have much in common and there is no denying the fact that of all print making techniques this is the one that best rendered his idea.

Despite a legend that is hard to kill, it was only after he had returned to France, namely late in 1893, that he did his first woodcuts. They were ten illustrations for the ten chapters of his *Noa Noa*. All in all Gauguin produced some forty woodcuts, which utterly revolutionized the technique formerly employed. He took novel, unorthodox means to work up his blocks. His equipment—needles, emery paper, gouge, pen-knife and razor—astonished other wood engravers. So did his choice of wood. At a time when all other artists used nothing but end wood, Gauguin took any ordinary plank and, like Albrecht Dürer, worked it up parallel to the grain.

The woodcut entitled *Nave Nave Fenua* (Delightful Land) went through four states. A commentary written by the Hungarian painter, József Rippl-Rónai, on the back of a proof of the second state, now in the Lessing J. Rosenwald Collection in the National Gallery of Art in Washington, proves that this second state was executed early in 1894. Consequently, the first state might date back to December 1893. This commentary is also valuable because it tells us that as Gauguin wanted to give Rónai a proof of the print he produced it in a very primitive manner in the latter's presence. This is how he proceeded. Having selected a sheet of paper, he laid it on his bed. Then he took the woodblock, inked it, placed it over the paper and put all his weight on it. This explains the irregularities one observes in some of Gauguin's prints, like the one reproduced here—a proof of the fourth state, which was executed with color blocks that the artist printed himself.

Nave Nave Fenua, 1894.
Woodcut in three colors, 35.4×20.4 cm.
Bibliography: M. Guérin, pl. 27.
Galerie Paul Prouté (formerly O'Connor Collection.)

Nave Nave Femia

Maillol's drawing is the drawing of a sculptor, namely three dimensional. Where the human figure is concerned, it has been demonstrated again and again by Daumier, Rodin, Despiau and a host of others—to mention only artists of modern times—that it is sculptors who render it best in drawings and engravings. The reason is that their work, compared with that of mere draughtsmen, has an additional dimension: the third dimension that renders volume.

Comparisons have often been drawn between Rodin and Maillol to show that, though they greatly admired each other, they were poles apart. It is in fact clear to see, when one examines their work, that the art of the former, always in movement, often restless and harassed, expresses what one might define with the single word dynamism. That of the latter, instead, has a tranquil, stable balance which makes it, in a word, static. Maillol offers us the proof that a great sculptor can also be restful. He restored to its relaxed calm the human body which Rodin had tortured and racked. Rodin's sculpture, with its violent emotion and stormy sensuality, is indeed a long way from the quiet, voluptuous calm, the happy, flowery sensuality, the blooming health of Maillol's work.

By birth, character and education, Aristide Maillol was a typical product of the Mediterranean. All his art is impregnated with the ideal of Greece and the atticism of France, and it was to the female form divine, as a sort of permanent homage, that he devoted his most important work. He did a great many female figures, either nude or lightly draped.

My choice fell on the lithograph reproduced here because, in my opinion, it is one of the finest examples of his graphic work besides being very typical of an artist whose aim was to give pleasure. The woman's splendid figure, the plastic beauty of her pose as, slightly twisted, she veils her nakedness after her bath, the delicate modeling of the pencil strokes, make this print a resounding success. With what consummate artistry Maillol has rendered the smooth curve of the neck under the thick knot of fair hair, the roundness of the beautiful shoulders that rise above a divine form worthy of Ceres or Pomona!

This lithograph was drawn on the stone by Maillol in 1924. There were two states, but the second differs from the first only in the presence of the artist's monogram drawn on the stone. This was erased after the master printer Duchâtel had pulled the entire edition for the publisher Edmond Frapier. After a few trial proofs there were seventy prints of the first state—thirty-five in sanguine, including the one reproduced here, and thirty-five in black—and a hundred and seventy-five of the second state. One hundred and twenty-five of the latter were inserted in the album *Maîtres et Petits Maîtres d'Aujourd'hui* published by Frapier in February 1925. Instead of signing his lithographs with his full name, Maillol marked them with his initials in pencil.

Woman from the Back, Draped, 1924.
Lithograph in sanguine, 27.8 × 12.9 cm. First state. No. 1/35.
Published by E. Frapier, Paris 1925.
Private Collection.

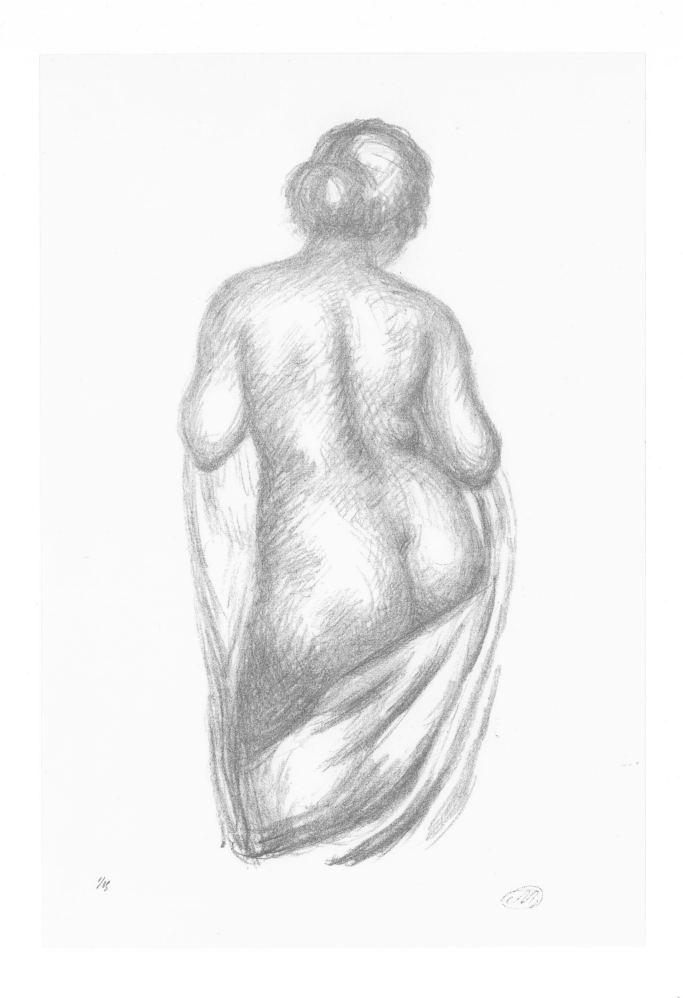

1/85

In 1892 Paul Signac discovered an unpretentious little port victualed by an ancient freighter from Marseilles. It was Saint-Tropez. Charles Vildrac has left us a description of its harbor with the fishing smacks dwarfed by the huge lateen sail of the tartans loaded with sand and, at vintage time, the quays stacked high with casks.

Signac was so happy at his discovery that he told all his friends about it and they came to Saint-Tropez in droves. The first to arrive were the other adepts of the "Divisionist" movement—Maximilien Luce, Cross (whose real name was Delacroix) and Théo Van Rysselberghe. Then came Henri Manguin, who in 1905 painted a picture entitled *The Fourteenth of July at Saint-Tropez* and stayed on the shore of the gulf right up to the end of his life; Henri Matisse, who settled at Sainte-Maxime; and Pierre Bonnard, the great yet modest Bonnard who became so fond of a part of the country that lay close to L'Estaque, which was celebrated by Cézanne, Braque and Derain. Later arrivals were Charles Camoin, who sold his villa there to Dunoyer de Segonzac in 1926; Segonzac himself, who arrived for the first time in 1908 with his friends the painters Boussingault and Luc-Albert Moreau and today is still loyal to Saint-Tropez though sixty years have passed; Albert Marquet, who lovingly transposed to his canvas the natural light, the intimate, discreet local color that we admire in his magnificent landscapes; and after them Lebasque, Jean Puy, Edouard Valtat and many, many more.

Saint-Tropez was not the only port Signac "discovered." As a tireless navigator, he discovered a great many others—from Holland to Corsica. In 1929 I went on a holiday with my father and remember coming across Signac at Lézardrieux, a charming little port on the north coast of France. I was still very young in those days and was hard put to it to recognize the artist I had met so often in Paris, in the Rue de Seine where we both lived. It was not easy to distinguish him from the Breton sailors as he sauntered along the quays where he painted his splendid watercolors. Signac was very fond of local color, which he rendered scrupulously and with infinite tenderness, poetry, and light in oils and watercolor. And also, as you can see here, in his prints, the finest of which sing the praises of Saint-Tropez. The lithograph reproduced here was executed in 1898 for the third volume of Vollard's *Album des Peintres-Graveurs*. It was printed by Clot and published in one hundred signed and numbered copies in addition to a small number of trial proofs. The design was based on notes jotted down from nature. A thousand touches of color sparkle from a thousand tiny facets to enable the eye to capture the optical blending in the nascent state and so produce what Signac aimed at, namely "the most harmonious, luminous and colorful result."

Saint-Tropez Harbor, 1898.
Color lithograph, 43.5 × 33.2 cm, No. 61/100.
Published by Vollard.
Collection Marcel Lecomte, Paris.

n° 61

P. Signac

When Munch stayed in Paris for the first time—it was in 1885—he was greatly impressed by the Rembrandts in the Louvre. After he returned in 1889 he was chiefly interested in Van Gogh, Seurat, Gauguin and Lautrec. In 1895 he stayed in Paris again and in the following year, under the influence of the lithographic printer Auguste Clot, did some color lithographs and his first woodcuts. Clot's uncanny skill has already been stressed in the note on Renoir's *Standing Nude* and his encounter with Edvard Munch was an important event in the history of print making. It was the time when the lithographs that revolutionized graphic art by the introduction of color were being produced in Clot's workshop. The revolutionary innovation consisted in the fact that it was the painters who chose the colors, with the result that the sheets printed by Clot and the master printers who followed in his footsteps were not reproductions but genuine works of art. All the great painter-engravers who worked with Ancourt, Stern, Clot and Lemercier executed color prints in their workshops, some of which turned out to be the first important products of the twentieth century in this field. Munch was one of those who took the most passionate interest in engraving. He too did wonderful lithographs and woodcuts that are quite extraordinary; unfortunately they are extremely rare and not as famous as they deserve to be. They include a number of masterpieces—*Jealousy I* and *II, Sick Child, August Strindberg, Moonlight* (plate p. 33), *In the Woods* (printed first by Lemercier in Paris, later by Lassaly in Berlin), *Self Portrait* 1895, *Madonna* 1895, *Large Nude with Red Hair* 1901, *Eva Mudocci* 1903, *A Man and a Woman Embracing* 1905, *The Death of Marat*—and many other masterly plates.

Munch's discovery of Gauguin's woodcuts was also an event of capital importance. Between them

—Gauguin late in 1893, Munch in 1896 on the verge of the twentieth century—they revolutionized wood engraving. Their impact was incalculable, for they reinstated side wood in the place of end wood, which had lost itself in a welter of insipidity. Munch loved wood for its own sake and utilized the grain of the board in his composition with masterly skill. He knew how to exploit nature's handiwork, guide it, and come to terms with it. He took pleasure in printing broad, uncut, veined areas to obtain ribbed, colored grounds. A magnificent example of this can be observed in the print reproduced here. Munch was fascinated by women's hair and gave it an important place in *Madonna, Vampire, Jealousy, Sick Child, Woman on the Beach, Woman, Large Nude with Red Hair, Eva Mudocci,* and many other plates.

For the last state of his masterly *A Man's Head in a Woman's Hair* he did two blocks. One was cut in several pieces for printing in various colors. They were engraved in 1896 and this proof was printed by Munch in person in 1900.

A Man's Head in a Woman's Hair, 1896–1900.
Woodcut in three colors, 55.1 × 38.2 cm.
Bibliography: G. Schiefler, Berlin 1907, pl. 80*b*.
Private Collection.

Munch's graphic *œuvre* comprises over eight hundred prints, among which color lithographs and woodcuts take pride of place. It must not, however, be forgotten that he also did some very fine etchings. Indeed his first encounter with print making was through engraving on copper. To start with, he mastered the drypoint, then went on to etching, line engraving and, lastly, aquatint. In each of these media he produced some very fine prints, such as *Death and the Young Girl, Vampire, Sick Child* (of which he also did a magnificent lithograph after his oil painting), *Moonlight* (a splendid drypoint and aquatint), *The Kiss, Man and Horse* (a delightful etching of a snowbound landscape), to mention but a few.

In some of Munch's prints we find a human figure, male or female, standing or seated in a dark room close to a window that lets in the cold light of the moon. All the rest of the print is in shadow. This shadow was obtained in different ways—either by the aquatint process or by line engraving with hatching and cross-hatching, sometimes by a combination of the two.

One of the proofs of the woodcut reproduced here was inscribed by Munch himself with the title *Night and Moonlight*, like his painting in the National Gallery in Oslo, whose composition closely resembles that of the print. It is one of the finest engravings he ever did. While the edition was being printed in Clot's workshop Munch pulled a number of proofs himself. Some are in two colors, some in three. Those in four colors, like the one reproduced here, were printed in 1901 and have unfortunately become extremely rare.

The great themes of Munch's paintings recur in his graphic works. In his lithographs and woodcuts, both in color and in black and white, he succeeded in rendering his idea with a terseness that gives the image a cogency which often excels that of the painting. In France Munch is not so well known as he should be and some people have said that his preoccupation was literary rather than painterly, but that charge does not stand up to a serious scrutiny of his graphic work. He was a friend of August Strindberg and Stéphane Mallarmé and one of the greatest painter-engravers of the twentieth century. Unfortunately his prints have become far too rare and seldom appear on the market. This is not surprising for he bequeathed over 15,000 to the City of Oslo. The fact that they are concentrated in Norway makes it very difficult to organize exhibitions in other countries. This is one of the factors that explain how it is that the great French public continues to ignore the work of an artist who, after Gauguin, did so much to broaden the scope of wood engraving and was one of the fathers of modern Expressionism.

Night and Moonlight, 1896–1901.
Woodcut in four colors, 40.3 × 47.3 cm.
Bibliography: G. Schiefler, Berlin 1907, pl. 81*d*.
Private Collection.

Between them, Toulouse-Lautrec and Daumier were responsible for the finest ensemble of lithographs that have ever been produced. The former's life was so short that he could not equal even one tenth of the latter's splendid output. But for ten years he took a passionate interest in print making and found expression in three hundred and seventy prints that provide ample proof of the force of his draughtsmanship and of his interest in media which, like so many other painters, he found no less important than painting. Lautrec was a born draughtsman and it was clear to see that sooner or later he would take up engraving. At the start lithography seemed to be the most direct method of doing so without abandoning the pencil. Moreover, Daumier, Redon and Degas had brought lithography to the peak of perfection. Degas was Lautrec's "god." With Daumier Lautrec had more than one trait in common. The attitude of the two great Expressionists towards the importance of landscape in art, which they both considered quite secondary, is worth quoting. "The face alone exists!" cried Lautrec, when in his presence someone extolled the artistic interest of landscape. As for still life, they ignored its very existence. Daumier's motto : "One must belong to one's age" was echoed by Lautrec's "Ah! Life. . . ." And, like Daumier, Lautrec displayed in his lithographs a certain seamy side of life with a realism that has never been equalled.

In 1891 Lautrec's very first lithograph—*Ball in the Moulin-Rouge*, which burst into blossom on the walls of Paris—made him famous overnight. The two actors he portrayed were widely known as "La Goulue" and "Valentin le Désossé" (Boneless Valentine). "La Goulue" was a "creature of lust and pleasure", a sensational, frenetic dancer, no less fascinating than lascivious. Lautrec, overstimulated and entranced, could not keep his eyes off her and studied her every move. He also studied "Valentin", who was crazy about dancing and every night at the Moulin-Rouge, without a fee, adopted hieratic, rhythmic poses to offset the amazing evolutions improvised by his partner. By day the extraordinary young man called himself Renaudin and worked as a bill collector for his brother, who was a notary. He was enormously tall and thin, and his agility was only displayed by his long legs while his torso remained motionless. Physically, he was the opposite of the cripple Lautrec, who was inevitably fascinated by him.

When Lautrec did this lithograph in 1894, "Valentin" was still dancing in the Moulin-Rouge but "La Goulue" was there no longer. So the artist redrew the characters of the poster from memory. The man is just as impassive as ever and the fair-haired girl seems to have calmed down considerably as she waltzes in his arms. The lithograph was first printed in an edition of one hundred copies before lettering which forms the first state. It was used later as the title page of a piece of music. What splendid evidence of Lautrec's genius as a draughtsman and of his passionate interest in the human face!

La Goulue and Valentin, 1894.
Lithograph in black and white, 31 × 25 cm.
Bibliography: L. Delteil, pl. 71; J. Adhémar, pl. 77.
Private Collection.

We have already seen how Lautrec that extraordinary draughtsman approached engraving through lithography. It should be pointed out that if his choice was determined by the natural development of a draughtsman who, after using an ordinary lead pencil on paper, went on to use a lithographic crayon on stone, that was not the only reason. When, as we shall see later, Degas initiated Suzanne Valadon, whose specialty was also drawing, in print making he preferred to start with soft-ground etching. In both media the pencil can be used as the engraver's tool and consequently they make it easy for a draughtsman to take the plunge. But Degas had a copperplate press, not a lithographic press, in his studio. Besides which, Lautrec and Valadon had from the outset different aims in view. He wanted to reach a public far vaster than an exhibition could—the public of the street. That is why he so gladly accepted the commission for a poster for the Moulin-Rouge. And lithography was the only medium which could overcome the difficulty that commission implied. Moreover, it would have been no easy matter for him, as a painter, to take in hand the burin right away without any previous training. Besides which, in 1895 etching, a medium that tempted him later, was passing through a period of lethargy. Since Cadart's death it had been employed exclusively by pure engravers and there was not a single gifted practitioner among them. Lastly, art critics like Mellerio and Roger Marx, dealers like Kleinmann and Sagot, publishers like Vollard, took a passionate interest in lithography, both in color and in black and white, and urged painters to apply themselves to it.

Thus in 1897 Vollard asked Lautrec for a color lithograph for his second *Album des Peintres-Graveurs*. It turned out to be one of his last color prints and the finest of them all. Lautrec told Vollard: "I shall do a brothel girl for you." But just then he started to be haunted by memories of his childhood. He saw once again in his mind's eye the ancient Hôtel du Bosc at Albi, the horses and the carriages. He experienced once again the morning drives through the countryside under a pure blue sky and a sun that cast a magic spell over all nature. So what he sent Vollard was something entirely unexpected—this trap or dog-cart in teak, something very typical of the period. The masterly composition of the lithograph leads the eye irresistably towards that happy horizon of youth and sunshine. And every detail of the perspective chosen by the artist tends towards the same direction—the trotting horse, the turning wheels, the silhouette of the loping dog, and the lines of the landscape. Never before had Lautrec achieved so daring a simplification and distribution of his colors. The whole edition numbered a hundred copies besides a few trial proofs that are extremely rare.

This print is considered one of the greatest masterpieces of color lithography.

The Dog-cart, 1897.
Lithograph in nine colors, 40 × 52 cm, No. 12/100.
Bibliography: L. Delteil, pl. 219; J. Adhémar, pl. 322.
Galerie R. and G. Michel, Paris.

Asked one day if there was nothing he regretted in his life, Lautrec replied: "Horses." His whole youth, before and even after the two accidents at fourteen and fifteen years of age that left him a cripple, was spent in the midst of horses—horses that belonged to his parents, his uncles, his cousins or his friends. Before the accidents he adored riding and there was no worse punishment than to deprive him of that pleasure. One of his father's friends, the animal painter René Princeteau, often painted horses, and ever since his earliest childhood drawing had been young Lautrec's second love. The margins of his copybooks were filled with caricatures, with portraits of his parents or his friends, with drawings of animals wild and tame, and above all of horses. In art he found an escape and Princeteau became his first teacher. At that time the horse was the subject to which he devoted most time, just as it became the dominant theme during his last years. Towards the end of his short life—and you may recall that Lautrec, like Van Gogh, was only thirty-seven when he died—the horse was the essential theme of his artistic production. Between 1897 and 1900 he did nineteen lithographs of horses, among them *Horse and Collie* (L. Delteil 208; J. Adhémar 259), *The Tandem* (L. D. 218; J. A. 260), *Horsewoman and Dog* (L. D. 285; J. A. 289), the extraordinary *Old Horse* (L. D. 224; J. A. 300), *The Trainer* (L. D. 172; J. A. 361), *The Paddock* (L. D. 280; J. A. 364), *The Jockey*, which Marcel Guérin more correctly entitled *Trial Gallop* (L. D. 279; J. A. 365), and the last, *Jockey Going to the Starting Post* (L. D. 282; J. A. 363), which Lautrec left unfinished because he died before deciding the shade of the grass.

About 1899 Pierrefort, a publisher in the Rue Bonaparte, commissioned a set of lithographs on *Racing* which he planned to bring out as a double set—in color and in black and white. Lautrec's illness and death prevented him from finishing the set. *The Jockey* was the only one executed: one hundred prints in black and white and the same number in color, of which twelve were on Japanese vellum. By that time he had given up going to the races, so *The Jockey*, *The Paddock* and his last work, *The Jockey Going to the Starting Post*, were done from memory.

What a splendid work this is, with the horse distorted by perspective, the jockey standing in his stirrups, his head sunk between his shoulders, and the identical posture of the second jockey in the middle distance to add point to the action and the surge towards the post, which we can just descry after the last bend in front of the mills on the far horizon!

Masterly draughtsmanship, careful selection of the printers, constant supervision of the impression, destruction of mediocre proofs, a passionate love of lithography: these are Lautrec's outstanding traits as a print maker. They explain the enormous popularity of his graphic work.

The Jockey, 1899.
Lithograph in six colours on Japanese vellum, 51 × 36 cm.
Bibliography: L. Delteil, pl. 279; J. Adhémar, pl. 365.
Private Collection.

Maurice Utrillo's mother had an exceptional talent for drawing, and when she first showed Toulouse-Lautrec her sketches he admired them wholeheartedly. They were done under the impact of an urge that Suzanne—her Christian name was really Marie-Clémentine—felt when she began to associate with the painters of the Butte Montmartre as a model after the trapeze accident that brought her career as an acrobat to an end. The story is well known. Lautrec, who was very fond of practical jokes, had tacked on the wall of his studio a few of his young model's sketches and found it amusing to ask his friends to name the author. They spontaneously mentioned the greatest draughtsmen of that day—Degas, Steinlen, even Van Gogh—and could hardly believe their ears when they were told the truth. One of them, the sculptor Bartholomé, was so enthusiastic that he decided to show the drawings to Degas. This marked the beginning of a great friendship. Unlike Renoir, Lautrec, Van Gogh, Steinlen and Puvis de Chavannes, Degas did not take Suzanne for his model. He did something far better : he gave her advice and lessons, particularly in the matter of engraving. I may also mention that he was the first to buy her work. A drawing in red chalk by Suzanne Valadon long adorned the wall of his dining room. In the end he told her : "You are one of us." Only those who know what Degas was really like can appreciate the full value, the true significance of these congratulations, lessons, purchases, this esteem, this exhibiting of her work. They reveal what he thought of the girl he called "Maria, that devil of a woman, that genius of drawing."

It was in 1895 that Degas initiated Suzanne Valadon in engraving in his studio. The master was anxious to make things as easy for her as possible, so he began by teaching her the technique of soft-ground etching. From the very start he realized his pupil's strong personality and uncompromising artistry. Knowing that she would never take the easy way, he quietly withdrew into the background and let her have her head. He would have greatly appreciated what she said later, after she had become a painter : "Never bring me as a sitter a woman who wants something pleasant and pretty. I would disappoint her right away."

When she had learnt soft-ground etching Suzanne Valadon took up drypoint; she pulled the prints herself but did not care about drawing attention to them. It was not till 1932 that a set of eighteen sheets—they were printed by Daragnès—brought her to the attention of the general public, as Claude Roger-Marx tells us in his preface to the set.

Her incisive line captures pose and movement searchingly and truthfully, with no care for "prettiness." What interested her were the things she saw round about her every day—her models, her son Maurice, her servant Catherine. Though the drypoint reproduced here from a proof she gave Degas is dated 1910 in Suzanne Valadon's own hand, it shows us Catherine drying Maurice after his bath.

Woman Drying a Child, 1910.
Drypoint and colored wash, 30.6 × 21.9 cm.
Bibliography: C. Roger-Marx, pl. 16.
Private Collection.

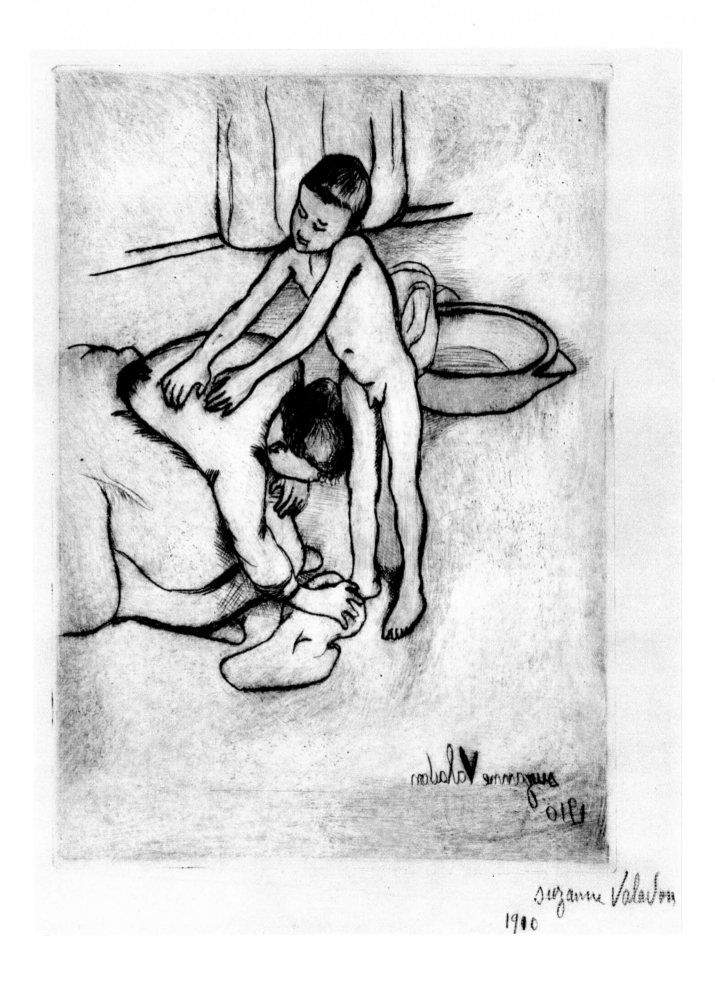

This splendid lithograph is the seventh of the series entitled *Scenes of Paris Life* that Vollard commissioned from Bonnard and published in 1899. Today the suite is very rare indeed, but as late as 1939 only half the edition of one hundred copies had been sold. It comprises twelve plates plus a frontispiece and was printed by Clot after Bonnard had studied and carried out experiments on the decomposition of colors.

Ambroise Vollard was a highly intelligent art dealer and won lasting fame by breaking through the bounds of his trade and bringing out the handsomest books published during the first half of the twentieth century as well as sets of original engravings. He was the first to approach contemporary painters and ask them to do color lithographs on subjects of their own choice. That is how Maurice Denis came to do his twelve prints on *Love*, Ker Xavier Roussel his *Landscapes*, Renoir his *Women and Portraits*, Vuillard his *Interiors* and Bonnard his *Scenes of Paris Life*.

Vollard's new departure opened up a vast range of possibilities and greatly interested the major painters of the period, notably the Nabi group, who were the true prophets where color lithography was concerned. Following in the footsteps of the Goncourt brothers, who had taken a passionate interest in Japanese colored woodcuts and made a great fuss about them, the Nabis became ardent admirers and collectors of those works. Bonnard was nicknamed "le Nabi très japonnard" (the very Japanese Nabi) and his first lithographs, after the famous *France-Champagne* poster that made such an impression on Toulouse-Lautrec, were inspired by those Japanese prints (*Family Scenes*, Roger-Marx, 2 and 4).

There was unfortunately no possibility of reproducing all thirteen prints of the series here, but they are all so fine that choosing one was no easy matter. *Street Corner* (R.-M. 58) and *The Triumphal Arch* (R.-M. 67) might have claimed the right to be included in this book instead of *The Costermonger*. If in the end I chose this print it was on account of the dog on the right, which is a little miracle, and the yellow tint that fills the print with sunlight like a Paris street on a fine spring day—a Paris street, with its horses and carriages and the crowded sidewalk in the background, over which an awning casts a translucent golden shade.

Bonnard used a paintbrush for the preliminary study or the definitive design of many of his lithographs. *The Costermonger*, which has five colors, was done entirely with the brush. That great connoisseur, Maître Maurice Loncle, had in his collection a splendid wash drawing which was a study for *House on the Courtyard* (R.-M. 59), another print of the same series. It shows with what care Bonnard prepared his lithographs.

The Costermonger, 1899.
Lithograph in five colors, 28.5 × 34 cm.
Bibliography: C. Roger-Marx, pl. 63.
Private Collection.

This is Bonnard's masterpiece and one of the finest color lithographs ever made. It demonstrates, once again, the immense superiority of the painter-engraver over the pure engraver. Only a painter could have produced a print of such quality.

I owe a debt of gratitude to M. Henri Petiet, who has always shown me great friendship and given me excellent advice. It was thanks to him that I was able to acquire this splendid specimen, which the owner gladly let me have on account of my enthusiasm for it. Need I insist on the joy I felt at the time and the constant pleasure this print has given me through the years. Observe its beautiful colors—the splendid bright red of the child's little train, which contrasts magnificently with the brick red of the table, the sumptuous tone of the lampshade, which sounds a chord deep down in our soul. Admire the abstract handling of the ground, which is treated overall in a very delicate, muffled tone that sets off the childish scene, and the matness—Bonnard's "delectable matness," which was so warmly praised in his paintings by his friend Thadée Natanson and which he succeeded in transposing to this lithograph, whose colors have the muffled tones of pleasant family life.

This print demanded five stones for the five colors chosen by the artist. It is said to have been printed in about 1897 but in my opinion it was executed later, perhaps in 1901 or 1902. This opinion rests on two arguments. First, the handling is more highly developed than in Bonnard's other lithographs, including his *Scenes of Paris Life*. Secondly, Vollard planned to use it in a third *Album des Peintres-Graveurs* together with plates by other artists, among them Picasso. But it is a well known fact that the first print Picasso executed in France was *The Frugal Meal*, which dates from 1904, and that Vollard first met Picasso in 1901.

In connection with *Child with Lamp*, as with many other of his lithographs, for instance *Boating* and *The Little Laundress*, Bonnard has left evidence to show how conscientious he was, namely in the experiments in color research he carried out in the printer's workshop, especially on the lamp, until he was entirely satisfied with the result.

This masterpiece by the man who illustrated Paul Verlaine's *Parallèlement* is the culminating point of a graphic *œuvre* which, like that of Toulouse-Lautrec, Redon and Picasso, counts among the most important of the last hundred years.

Child with Lamp, 1901.
Lithograph in five colors, 33.5 × 46 cm.
Bibliography: C. Roger-Marx, pl. 43.
Private Collection.

When Roussel was a pupil at the Lycée Condorcet in Paris he met Maurice Denis and, more important still, Edouard Vuillard. The latter became his best friend and brother-in-law. The two young men began their careers as painters by studying in Maillard's studio. After that they attended lessons at the Académie Julian, where they made friends with Pierre Bonnard with whom they formed an inseparable trio that lasted as long as they lived. In those days Roussel painted in somber colors.

Two important events cleared his vision and led him to adopt the bright style of his mature period typified by cloudless blue skies that sang the gay mythology of grace and youth. First, in 1889 Paul Sérusier, who was student-in-charge at Julian's, came back from Pont-Aven, where he had met Gauguin towards the end of the previous year. That meeting was an event of capital importance because Sérusier, a theoretician, passed on Gauguin's style and ideas to all the other young painters at the school. Incidentally, Sérusier brought back from Brittany the famous "talisman" he had painted in adjacent planes of unmixed primary colors on the lid of a cigar box in the Bois d'Amour. The young artists, who were joined by Henri Gabriel Ibels, Paul Ranson, Félix Vallotton and Aristide Maillol, formed the group that the poet Cazalis called the Nabis, from the Hebrew word for prophet. It was not long, however, before the three friends tired of Sérusier's theories and, freeing themselves from the influence of Gauguin, set up a splinter group of their own. That was the time when Vallotton, who just then was chiefly concerned with woodcuts in black and white, publicized in Switzerland the artistic ideas and output of Bonnard, Vuillard and Roussel.

The second event that definitively brightened Roussel's somber palette was the trip he made to the South of France with Maurice Denis, during which he met Cézanne, who died in that very same year. The dazzling light of the Mediterranean coast gave Roussel a bright, serene and joyful vision. This brightness and serenity are obvious in the lithograph reproduced here. It belonged to a series entitled *Landscapes* that was commissioned by Vollard in 1898. The set should have totaled twelve plates but was unfortunately broken off after the sixth.

Ker Xavier Roussel was unassuming as a man and full of life as an artist. He was fond of depicting the bucolic scenes of pagan mythology set in bright landscapes where one would not be surprised to see Daphnis and his beloved Chloé appear at any moment in all the splendor of their youth and happiness.

Woman in a Striped Dress, 1900.
Lithograph in four colors, 21.4 × 32 cm.
Bibliography: J. Salomon, pl. 16.
Private Collection.

This magnificent lithograph and the one that follows are often viewed as forming a pair. Actually the only justification for this theory is that both represent children with their mother or nurse against a landscape background. But what of that ? Taken separately they are quite self-sufficient for each is a work of the first importance in its own right.

The print reproduced on the opposite page shows a walk in the Tuileries Gardens in Paris and a little girl accompanied by her imposing nurse running to meet a group of women and children. Viewed by itself, this group is a little miracle of line and color. Pigeons strut in the foreground, while in the distance we can see some tiny figures limned in a delightful shade of blue that sets off the unusual green of the lawn and establishes the perspective of the flat garden, at once spacious and intimate, which differs so greatly in character from the other Paris parks.

If we forget for a moment *Seated Dressmaker* (Roger-Marx 13), of which a hundred copies were printed in ochre and blue in 1895 for the *Album de la Revue Blanche, The Tuileries Gardens* may be considered Vuillard's first color print. As so often happens where great artists are concerned, it was already a masterpiece.

This lithograph in five colors was printed by Auguste Clot, using five different stones, in 1896 for Vollard's first *Album des Peintres-Graveurs*, which was published in an edition of one hundred copies containing twenty-two plates each.

Vuillard did a couple of preliminary studies in pastels and watercolors. After that he executed the lithograph, for which he did two states and a number of trial proofs for the colors, notably the green of the lawn. This goes to show how conscientiously that great artist worked. A great artist but a modest one, for he later said to the critic Claude Roger-Marx : "You were wrong to write that I was a great painter : I may have been a good one."

No better praise of Vuillard's graphic work could be imagined than what André Masson said, namely that he gave his color lithographs the noblest quality of all : they neither copy nor imitate paintings. This quality is intrinsic to his handling of the medium—a wash of incomparable subtlety over a drawing done solely with the lithographic crayon and as a rule in muted tones.

In other words, the most discriminating of French colorists was also the most refined of French lithographers. He achieved the utmost discretion. For instance, in the print that served as frontispiece for the portfolio of twelve lithographs entitled *Paysages et Intérieurs* he did for Vollard, he used only two colors—violet-gray and emerald green—yet succeeded in producing an effect of incomparable richness. Masson formulated a fundamental truth as regards engraving when he said : "Vuillard is well aware that the base is the paper and that one must know how to use this white or ivory ground as an essential color."

The Tuileries Gardens, 1896.
Lithograph in five colors, 30.9 × 43.2 cm.
Bibliography: C. Roger-Marx, pl. 28.
Private Collection.

Ambroise Vollard published this masterpiece by Vuillard in 1897 in his second *Album des Peintres-Graveurs*, which also contained Bonnard's *Boating* (Roger-Marx 41) and *Little Laundress* (R.-M. 42).

This lithograph too was printed in one hundred copies and Vuillard first made a quantity of experiments on the decomposition of colors, as he had done for *The Tuileries Gardens*. It went through three states and was printed in four colors—yellow, dark blue, beige-gray and red. In the third state, to which the print reproduced here belongs, the artist used a point to work over the sailor suit of the child who is being helped up after a fall, and so lower the tone of the foreground. It is one more proof that it takes a painter to achieve so felicitous a combination of unusual tonalities and difficult color harmonies. The yellow of the ground and the acid blue of the child's suit are quite out of the ordinary. They shock us at first but we are soon completely won over by their marvelous concordance. And the ball is really a splendid red. . . .

These two prints are so advanced for the period that one is amazed to discover that they were executed in 1895 and 1896. But not only the *avant-garde* attitude of the artist seemed unusual to his contemporaries : the procedure adopted by the publisher was no less so. Vollard had been deeply impressed by *L'Estampe originale* in 1893 and the *Album de la Revue Blanche* in 1895. He realized at once that it would be extremely interesting to publish portfolios of color lithographs specially commissioned from painters for that purpose. His was an unprecedented initiative (if we exclude Manet's *Polichinelle*, which was no great success.) It is true that ever since Senefelder invented lithography the medium had been employed for producing color prints, only however by second-rate artists for academic townscapes or for posters. These cannot bear comparison with those executed by Chéret or, better still, by the Nabis and Toulouse-Lautrec.

Strange to say, Vollard's portfolios were not at all appreciated by his contemporaries. The indifference with which they were received so discouraged both artists and publisher that the latter did not even complete his third portfolio. What a loss that was! Just imagine what masterpieces the Fauves, for instance, would have created in this medium!

Fifty years passed before the value of these two lithographs by Vuillard was recognized. Today, twenty years later—that is the usual time lag—they are extremely hard to come by because collectors all over the world are on the look-out for them and, once found, do not let go of them.

Children at Play, 1897.
Lithograph in four colors, 28 × 44.2 cm.
Bibliography: C. Roger-Marx, pl. 29.
Private Collection.

Like the large *Nude with Raised Arms* (Barr 63) and *Odalisque in a Net Skirt* (B. 107), this lithograph is one of the masterpieces of Matisse's graphic *œuvre*.

Matisse produced over six hundred prints and woman is the subject of most, if not all, of them. Copper, wood, linoleum and especially the lithographer's stone served his passion for rendering the female form and face. His sets of prints showing the same model in different poses are ample proof of what care he devoted to the study of the female figure. In *Plaisir de peindre*, André Masson has given us a very good account of how Matisse —whose drawings are so extraordinarily spirited— worked in the noblest sense of the word beforehand on innumerable sketches in pencil or charcoal. It was only after much practise, when he was sure of his stroke—what Masson called his "tender stroke" —that he tackled the definitive drawing. "It is to set grace free," said Matisse, "that I study so hard before doing a drawing. I never force anything on myself; on the contrary, I am like a dancer or an acrobat who begins his day with several hours of vital limbering-up exercises so that every part of his body obeys when, in public, he wants to render his feelings in a series of dance steps, fast or slow, or in an elegant pirouette."

He followed the same procedure in his many lithographs, where the linework of the definitive design is lively and free, with striking short-cuts achieved with almost virulent agility. This self-imposed sobriety proves that Matisse had perfectly assimilated the lesson learnt from his master Gustave Moreau : "In art the more elementary are the means, the more evident is the sensibility." This tallies with Manet's pithy maxim : "In art concision is necessity and elegance."

But, in contrast to this austere style of engraving, Matisse took pleasure in exaggerating the roundness of the forms and rendering the most diverse textures—wool, silk, fur and so on—as if to prove that his skill was not restricted to pure, true line and that he was capable of "finishing" a drawing in the sense a certain public demanded. However, there are times when these stylistic exercises come very close to affectation. The three prints mentioned at the beginning of this commentary are among Matisse's most finished lithographs, but they are far from incurring a slur of that sort. They are indeed genuine masterpieces.

In this "Bayadère" Matisse has treated the stone with an amazingly light hand. The grain of the skin, the roundness of the bosom, the sensuous curves of the arms and figure, are splendidly rendered, as are the iridescent fabrics of trousers and armchair that stand out against the fine black ground. These traits make the plate a masterpiece of draughtsmanship. It was printed in 1925; the edition comprised fifty copies plus a few artist's proofs.

The Bayadère Trousers, 1925.
Lithograph in black and white, 54.3 × 44 cm, No. 32/50.
Bibliography: Barr, pl. 64.
Collection Marcel Lecomte, Paris.

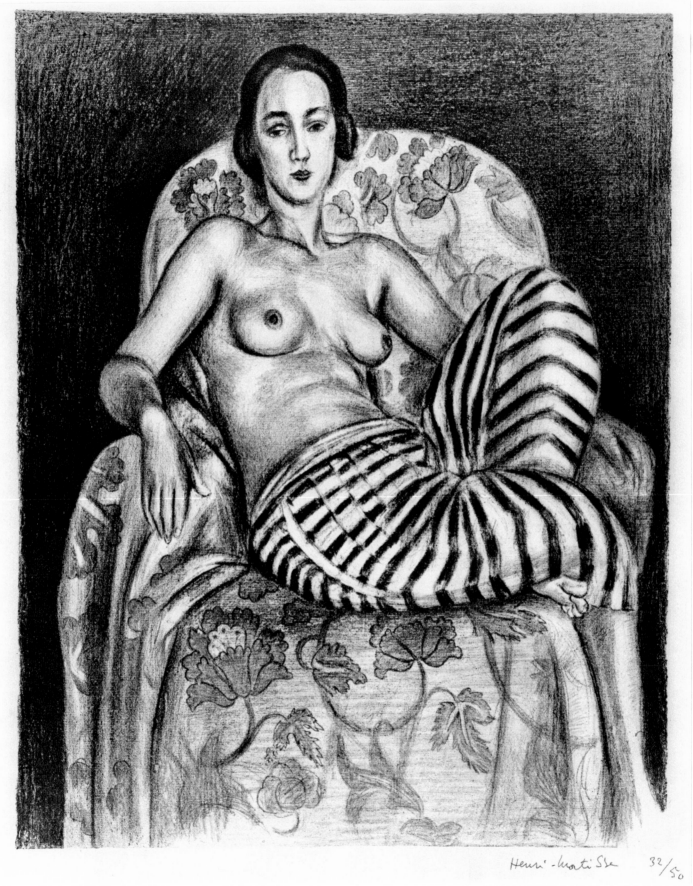

Henri-Matisse   32/50

53

"I have realized that the relentless labor of my life has been for the great human family, to which a fraction of the world's fresh beauty was to be revealed through my intermediary."

These noble words honor Matisse the man and the worker, who confessed that for sixty years he had worked twelve hours a day. Contemplating this magnificent lithograph, one sees how true they are. Here Matisse has found pleasure in dressing up his model in the gauziest of skirts and has stressed the exotism that served him as a pretext by adding an occasional table in pseudo-islamic style. The same model appears in many of his lithographs attired as a Persian, an Indian or a beauty from the *Arabian Nights*.

The lithograph was designed in 1929 and printed in fifty copies plus a number of artist's proofs. The reproduction that faces this page was made from the press proof annotated and signed in the artist's own hand. Its warm, luminous tones make it a truly beautiful print.

Matisse himself said: "My drawings generate light," and, according to Guillaume Apollinaire, "the *œuvre* of Henri Matisse is a fruit of dazzling light." What a splendid fruit the great master of twentieth-century painting has left us in this lithograph, which demonstrates once again his masterly skill as a draughtsman! When we examine it we feel for ourselves the vivid pleasure with which he drew this woman with a feather-light hand and rendered with an incomparable gradation of grays the fullness of the body and its voluptuous curves, the perfect roundness of the young bosom, the thistledown lightness of the net that ripples like a wisp of mist over the long, graceful thighs. What infinite care the artist has lavished on every detail of the body! Nor has he neglected the girl's face, whose subtle smile expresses an awareness that she is beautiful and an amused curiosity as to what that

beauty can achieve. It is clear to see that when he drew this plate Matisse took pleasure in the woman's figure and the flowers, which are sources of light. His interest waned when it came to tackling the setting and, as a result, the strict geometrical design of walls and floor lack warmth and radiance.

Matisse aimed at expressing his religious attitude —if one can call it that—towards life. And he said: "I cannot distinguish between what I feel about life and how I render that feeling. A drawing must have an expansive force that enlivens the things that surround it." When we look at this print in our own home—and for a print the atmosphere of one's home is far more favorable than that of a museum—we feel the expansive force that radiates from it and lights up the whole room.

Odalisque in a Net Skirt, 1929.
Lithograph in black and white, 28.9 × 37.7 cm. Press proof.
Bibliography: Barr, pl. 107.
Galerie Prouté, Paris.

Maurice Denis was also one of the Nabis, and in fact their spiritual father. He too, like Bonnard, Vuillard and Roussel, was commissioned by Vollard to do a set of twelve lithographs and a frontispiece in color. He took *Love* as his theme and Vollard published the portfolio in 1911. Undoubtedly, the finest of the thirteen prints is the frontispiece: it represents a nude woman seen from the back, who has just let her veil fall to her feet and is making a very pretty gesture with her raised arms. The same pose occurs in other engravings by Denis, notably in a delightful little woodcut entitled *Nude Woman from the Back*, as well as in *Bather on the Shore of a Lake*, which served as a frame for Stéphane Mallarmé's *Petit Air*:

"Quelconque une solitude

. . .

Dans l'onde toi devenue
Ta jubilation nue"

Denis started work on the set in 1892 and finished it in 1899. In the third print, *The Morning Bouquet, the Tears*, and the eleventh, *Life Becomes Precious and Prudent*, the scene is laid in a garden with a circular pool. The first of these two prints is an upright rectangle and the setting is almost the same as in the lithograph reproduced here, for which Denis drew the design on the stone about the same time, namely in 1897. *Reflection in a Fountain* was printed by Clot in a hundred copies, plus a few trial proofs, for Vollard's second portfolio.

Pierre Cailler, in his *catalogue raisonné* of Maurice Denis's graphic *œuvre*, says nothing of the various states of this print. I myself know of four. In the first state the seated woman's blouse is pure white; the glass door has five panes; the signature, M.A.U.D., is inscribed vertically on the wall, high up on the left; blue is the dominant color of the ground around the lawn and of the flower bed that frames the shrubbery under the trees in the distance. Then comes the proof reproduced here, which differs from the former in the toning down of the dominant blue on the ground and still more on the flower bed, where the dominant color is now rose; on the lawn the blades of grass are less distinct; the bather's breasts, eyes and mouth are more clearly drawn. In the third state the woman's blouse is dotted; the signature is written on the ground instead of on the wall; all the tints on the ground, the wall and the bushes have been recast; only two panes of the door can be seen; and the yellowish green of the foliage has been changed to green. Lastly, in the final state, as printed in the portfolios, the distinction between ground, lawn and flower bed is less sharp.

This lithograph is undoubtedly the finest print Denis ever did.

Reflection in a Fountain, 1899.
Lithograph in five colors, 41.7 × 25.6 cm. Second of four states.
Bibliography: P. Cailler, pl. 100.
Private Collection.

Georges Rouault's *Miserere* is often considered one of the masterpieces of twentieth-century graphic art. It was commissioned by Vollard after he had seen, in the artist's studio, a number of large wash drawings on the theme of the misery of the human condition, most of them inspired by World War I. Like all those who had lived through that period, Rouault was deeply scarred by his experience, and it was he who produced the most pathetic prints on that dreadful cataclysm.

Vollard and Rouault agreed at the start that the work would comprise two volumes of one hundred plates each, the first entitled *Miserere*, the second *War*. As Rouault explains in his Preface, a certain number of his drawings were transferred heliographically from the paper to the copperplates. These served him as a base for the execution between 1922 and 1926 of the large plates, each of which was printed in several states. For the purpose he employed various engraving techniques, such as etching and aquatint, and a quantity of different tools—needle, burnisher, paintbrush, emery paper and so on. Vollard tells us that one day he went to see how the work was getting on and got a shock when he saw what unorthodox tools Rouault used to work up his plates. When he voiced his surprise, this is what the artist replied: "The name of the process doesn't matter. I have a copperplate so I go for it hammer and tongs."

Nine years after Vollard's death Rouault got back his plates and in 1948 published *Miserere*, which he considered his artistic testament. He kept only fifty-eight of the plates engraved thirty-five years earlier. This is to be regretted for, after examining eighty-two, I can say that there were some very fine ones among those he eliminated. Rouault wrote the titles on some of the trial proofs and later, when the set was published, composed the definitive caption-title for each of the fifty-eight.

The print I have selected is the finest of them all. It was engraved in 1923. Rouault found inspiration in the circus for many of his paintings and engravings. Here the caption-title, *Who Isn't Made Up?*, is as terrifying as the print itself. There is no forgetting the clown's face as he smooths out his wry grin to ask us this question in reply to the one we rather thoughtlessly put to him. With his mournful head bent in compassion, a disenchanted half-smile on his lips, he casts at us a glance full of gentle, sad reproach that compels us to ponder on this work, which makes a lasting impression on the beholder. *Who Isn't Made Up?* is one of Rouault's greatest masterpieces.

The plates were printed by Jacquemin in Paris between 1922 and 1927 on Arches paper with Ambroise Vollard's watermark. The edition was limited to four hundred copies, after which Vollard had the plates scored.

Who Isn't Made Up?, 1923.
Brush and drypoint engraving, 56.6 × 42.9 cm.
Bibliography: Abbé Morel, pl.*VIII*; Kornfeld and Klipstein, pl. 50/8.
Published by L'Etoile Filante, Paris 1948.
Private Collection.

In 1965 a selection of Rouault's work was exhibited in the Galerie Charpentier in Paris. Robert Nacenta included in his catalogue an unpublished text by the artist, quoting a passage from the testament of Rouault's intimate friend, André Suarès: "No matter what shape my experience or my faith may take, I love Jesus and am loyal to all Christian beauty. It is the source of human kindness. Where it does not exist, barbarism with its bodyguards, pride and cruelty, the legates of Hell, is always close at hand. . . . Like all the children of God, I seek the Father's bosom and await the Paraclete." When we study Rouault's work we realize how deeply he must have felt these words. Religion provided the inspiration for one-third of his graphic *œuvre*.

Rouault is the most forceful of the Christian artists who have produced religious paintings in the twentieth century. The same is true of engravings as well. The foregoing text concerns one of the plates of his monumental *Miserere*. Of the fifty-eight prints comprised in that great series, twenty have religious themes. This concurs with the ratio of one to three I have just mentioned. A new power pervades the strikingly beautiful plates of this *chef-d'œuvre*. The artist has left aside the caricatural aspect he had stressed in his previous works and has rendered the human countenance with a terrifying expressionism. This is enhanced by the force of the black and the white, which he treats with amazing mastery. The painterly substance of these plates is so extraordinarily rich and forceful that one does not regret the precise linework of other artists. In their entirety these prints constitute a pitiless indictment of the human condition as bound by civilization. Some of them, however, are illuminated by Rouault's boundless compassion for mankind.

Rouault did several representations of the Crucifixion with two or three figures at the foot of the Cross. His graphic *œuvre* alone includes at least three lithographs and three copperplates on this scene, one of them in the *Miserere* suite. That reproduced here is the largest and the only one in color. It was engraved at Lacourière's in 1936 and printed in three hundred copies, one hundred and seventy five of them numbered, in 1946.

In this splendid print Rouault aimed at symbolizing all the pain men inflict on each other. The great artist was sensitive and compassionate towards the unfortunate and always felt close to the lowly. Like Daumier, he waxed violent in his condemnation of the stupidity and insensibility of the intelligentsia and the middle class, but he lacked Daumier's imperturbable good nature. This explains the tragic virulence of his *œuvre*, in which medieval spirituality blends with modern expressionism.

Crucifixion, 1936.
Aquatint in color, 64.8 × 49 cm, No. 67/175.
Bibliography: Kornfeld and Klipstein, pl. 41.
Private Collection.

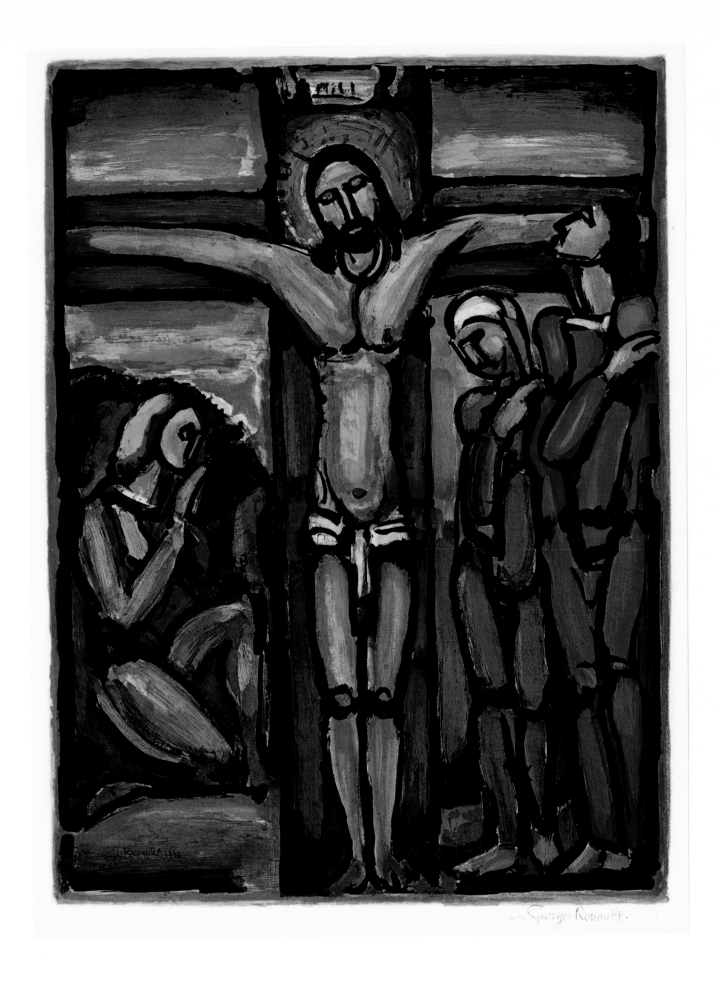

It was in the workshop of the master printer, Roger Lacourière, that Rouault was initiated into the beauties of the color aquatint. That was the year 1936. Four years earlier Picasso, who happened to drop in there—Prévert says he dropped in everywhere everyday as if the place was his—had discovered Lacourière and introduced him to Vollard. So it came about that, through the genius of several great artists, the initiative of certain publishers and the skill of the master printer, a set of illustrated books, which rank amongst the most beautiful of those printed in the twentieth century, was produced. Rouault accepted the task of executing a set of color aquatints for an edition of Baudelaire's *Fleurs du Mal* which was unfortunately never published. Twelve of the engravings are still extant, the finest being this *Seated Nude* (or *Nude in Side View*, Kornfeld 122) and *Christ in Profile* (see p. 65, K. 131). The other prints also have rich colors, recalling stained glass windows.

It is worth noting that when he was fourteen years old Rouault was placed as an apprentice in the workshop of a glass painter named Hirsch, who at that time was busy restoring medieval stained glass windows. Contact with that extraordinarily rich material left its mark on Rouault for the rest of his long life. This can be seen in his handwriting, his colors and a love of good craftsmanship that remained with him until his death. The period spent with Hirsch gave Rouault a thorough grounding in drawing and in the working up of colors and impasto. The skills he thus learnt when still a boy served him in his paintings and engravings. Familiarity with stained glass gave him a taste for the iridescence produced by the passage of light through colored glass and for the definition of his figures with heavy black contours.

The other ten prints of the series represent judges, fleshy or decrepit prostitutes, another very

fine head of Christ, and a Crucifixion. The last shows us Baudelaire's grave.

Before trying his hand at color aquatints, Rouault already, in 1926, done some etchings and aquatints in black and white for *Fleurs du Mal*. Though very interesting, these prints are not so fine as those of the third set I mentioned above. These latter, which are in color, deserve to be termed the summum of the artist's thought. They are more valid, sober and masterly. This is clear to see when we compare the three nudes in side view of the three sets. It is not a question of the difference between color and black and white—indeed, in a print color is seldom the most significant factor—but of the works themselves. The last of the three is a masterpiece; the others are stages, if not states, of the artist's thought.

Seated Nude, 1936.
Aquatint in color, 31.2 × 20.9 cm.
Published first by A. Vollard, later by H.-M. Petiet.
Bibliography: Kornfeld and Klipstein, pl. 122.
Private Collection.

This color aquatint also belongs to the *Fleurs du Mal* series and is, indeed, the finest of the set and one of the finest prints Rouault ever made. It is deservedly in great demand but this has been the case only in recent years. Before that these works were known only to a few initiates. When they finally appeared on the market they were received with growing admiration.

There are three different prints by Rouault depicting Christ in side view. The other two (Kornfeld 172/7 and 172/9) belong to the magnificent set of seventeen color aquatints for André Suarès's *Passion*, the handsomest book illustrated by Rouault after *Miserere* and *Le Cirque de l'Etoile Filante*. Their format is identical to a fraction of an inch and both are dated 1936. The one reproduced here is dated 1937. It may well be said that all three plates were engraved under the impact of the same inspiration and with the same technique. In one of those executed for *Passion* Christ faces left. In the other He faces right, as He does in the plate reproduced here. This last, which was done for *Fleurs du Mal*, is the finest of the three. But, unlike the three nudes we have just examined, which differ greatly in artistic value, the three busts of Christ are more homogeneous. Although the Christ of *Fleurs du Mal* towers above the others owing to the noble, commanding carriage of the head and the extraordinary expression of self-sacrifice, of suffering received and accepted, that radiates from the features rendered with slashing brush strokes on the copperplate. The effect is overpowering and one attempts in vain to discover how the artist succeeded in expressing such lofty sentiments. With a broad, flexuous, meandering stroke of the brush, which lacks any direct link with or resemblance to the lines that usually define the eyes, the cheekbones, the sunken jowls, he has clearly stated everything once and for all. It is not a mask but a living face; it is suffering man, it is Christ himself we are gazing at.

This plate is, in my opinion, one of George Rouault's three or four most significant prints. It is a typical product of a painter-engraver who, under the impact of his genius, has abandoned the usual tools of the pure engraver, tackled his copperplate in the throes of inspiration, and worked a miracle. Here too the colors are deep and sumptuous, and their beauty enhances that of this extraordinary work.

The twelve aquatints of this series were engraved between 1936 and 1938 and printed in two hundred and fifty copies on very handsome "Maillol" vellum. Rouault had fifty additional proofs pulled from the black plate alone.

Christ in Profile, 1937.
Aquatint in color, 32 × 21.5 cm.
Published first by A. Vollard, later by H.-M. Petiet.
Bibliography: Kornfeld and Klipstein, pl. 131.
Private Collection.

65

Boulogne Harbor

Albert Marquet, a native of Bordeaux, was attracted all his life long by large expanses of water, by the bustle of harbors and the calm of inland waterways. He painted splendid pictures on the Paris bridges (the Pont-Neuf, the Pont Saint-Michel, the Pont de Conflans), on the banks and quays of the Seine (the Quai Conti, the Quai des Grands-Augustins, the Quai du Louvre), in many seaports (Honfleur, Boulogne, Fécamp, Le Havre, La Rochelle, Les Sables d'Olonne, Audierne, Marseilles, Algiers, Tunis, Naples, Venice, Vigo, Sulina on the Danube, Galatz in Rumania, Hesness in Norway, Amsterdam, Stockholm, Hamburg), and on innumerable beaches. But this long list must not lead us to forget that Marquet also did some fine nudes and portraits. These latter reveal a vigorous handling and a psychological insight that earn him a place among the great specialists in this field. He also drew rapid sketches that are spirited and humorous. Matisse, who admired them greatly, said of Marquet : "He is our Hokusai."

Marquet's painting is calm, limpid, restful, as transparent as the vast stretches of water he loved so well. How different, in their modesty and simplicity, from the stormy seascapes and landscapes of Impressionists like Claude Monet, who too often ignored the calm beauty of a wind-still morning and the unrippled surface of a lake. We are all too apt to forget that Marquet was a precursor of Fauvism as early as 1897. Though his art "raises no problems," his reputation as a painter is spreading steadily and his mastery is being increasingly recognized.

Like all complete artists, Marquet did a lot of engravings, notably of Paris townscapes, of the banks of the Seine and of seaports. The lithograph reproduced here may perhaps be considered as his masterpiece. The stone was done about 1930 and seventy-five copies were printed. There is an oil painting on panel (measuring 33 × 41 cm) of the same port viewed from exactly the same spot, with the same tugboat moving away and the freighter berthed under the crane. The lithograph is printed on rice paper, which gives wonderful, velvety blacks, and pasted on to stronger paper. The subtle interplay of the ripples with the reflection of the smoke and sky renders to perfection the atmosphere of a seaport and makes this print a truly masterly work.

It is to be regretted that Marquet who, like Delacroix, made drawing his daily prayer, did not produce more numerous engravings. We feel the lack all the more when we admire the little figures, the portraits, the landscapes executed with such supreme authority and such delightful humor in brush and Indian ink. Had he done them on copperplate or lithographic stone he would have given us no less pleasure than have Bonnard and Toulouse-Lautrec.

Boulogne Harbor, *c.* 1930.
Lithograph, 28.7 × 38 cm, No. 8/75.
Private Collection.

8/75

marquet

Jacques Villon did his first color aquatint in 1899 with the assistance and advice of Eugène Delâtre, the famous copperplate printer who was responsible for the delightful color prints executed in the same medium by Mary Cassatt. By 1909, when Villon did *On the Pigs*, his last color aquatint before the large facsimile reproductions of 1922, he had used that technique for some sixty prints. Those works were long neglected but have now come into their own and are, indeed, highly appreciated and much sought after. Fine specimens that have kept their freshness because sheltered from direct sunlight, which is so bad even for prints in black and white, display splendid colors, transparent when pale, rich when dark, without violent contrasts but with an unrivaled range of subtle shades.

In these aquatints Villon treated a great variety of subjects—fun-fair scenes, life in military barracks drawn and engraved from memory, aggressive demonstrations, beach scenes in pale, diaphanous tints, smart Parisian women contemporaries of those portrayed in drypoint by Helleu, occasional genre scenes like the splendid plate of 1903 entitled *Cards* (Jacqueline Auberty and Charles Pérussaux 44) or the amazing *Nevers in Paris* of 1904 (A. and P. 55). *A Game of Backgammon* engraved in 1902 deserves to be called the finest of this series of aquatints. In quality it excells *Cards* though the latter, being better known, is more sought after.

Only thirty copies of *A Game of Backgammon* were printed. Five proofs were pulled of a first state with a plain background. Then Villon took the plate in hand again and designed the background as it appears in the reproduction on the opposite page. Eugène Delâtre printed twenty-five copies of this second state; they were all signed and numbered by the artist.

What Villon has depicted here is a family scene. The young woman on the left is his sister, Suzanne

Duchamp, who was also a painter and engraver. On the right is his brother, the painter Marcel Duchamp, who was a great chess player. Duchamp, one of the founders of the Dada movement, author of *Nude Descending a Staircase* and *The Bride Denuded by Her Bachelors (La Mariée mise à nu par ses Célibataires, même)* later joined the Surrealists and settled in the United States.

In the print reproduced here Villon touched up his sister's face with a pencil. The firm drawing, the harmonious distribution of the patches of color, the choice of the colors, the composition of the scene, the postures of the players, the extraordinary beauty of their faces, combine to give this work a leading place among the sixty or more color aquatints Villon produced between 1899 and 1909.

A Game of Backgammon, 1902.
Aquatint in color, 33.8 × 47.6 cm. Second state. No. 12/25.
Bibliography: Auberty and Pérussaux 37.
Collection Marcel Lecomte, Paris.

12/25   Jacques Villon

This masterly print is one of the finest Villon ever did. He engraved the plate a year before the famous Golden Section Exhibition that immediately preceded his conversion from analytical to synthetic Cubism.

For some years he had pondered intensely on the artistic "effervescence" in which he was living. During his Montmartre period, from 1898 to 1905, he had engraved topical subjects and produced sumptuous color aquatints. One of these we have just seen.

In 1905 Fauvism, a new movement based on the exaltation of color, suddenly burst like a bomb. In 1907, the year after Cézanne's death, an important retrospective show of that great master's work provided our young painter with a foundation, a substructure, on which to build up new theories. That was the year when, after discovering Negro art, Picasso and Braque invented Cubism. So one must not be surprised to see that Villon's engraving was gradually transformed in keeping with this revolutionary context. Little by little he abandoned genre scenes and color. In 1910 he gave up color entirely. From then on he was concerned solely with formal analysis and the vast, fascinating resources of black and white. The Pre-Cubist and Cubist engravings he produced at that time count among the masterpieces of his whole graphic *œuvre*. Indeed his Cubist engravings are unanimously considered the most important prints executed by any of the Cubist painters—superior even to those by Braque and Picasso.

Renée, the daughter of one of Villon's friends, was orphaned at a very tender age. Villon took her as his model for many drawings and engravings. The first prints in which she appears date from 1901. It was she who sat for the set of sixteen *Bain de Minne* prints and, in 1911, for four others of which the most important is the one reproduced here.

In this engraving Villon has kept the large format of some of his aquatints, thus giving it a still more commanding appearance. His skill with the drypoint enabled him to express himself with supreme authority, as we can see here. After first taking care of the volumes and sketching in long, sharp strokes the bust and arms of his young sitter—Renée must have been about eighteen years of age in 1911—the artist concentrated on the face. How splendidly he has rendered the apparently hostile expression of mute, obstinate disapproval, while letting us, with amazing mastery, glimpse in her eyes a hint of anxiety!

Only thirty copies were printed from this plate —not forty as is stated in the catalogue of Villon's graphic *œuvre*. In my eyes it is one of the finest engravings produced in the last hundred years and one of those that make an extraordinary, permanent effect on the beholder.

Renée Viewed from Three-Quarters, 1911.
Drypoint, 56 × 41 cm, No. 22/30.
Bibliography: Auberty and Pérussaux 181.
Private Collection.

20/30   Jaqu Villa

Yvonne D. from the Side

This work and *The Laid Table* are the two most sought after of all Villon's prints. It dates from 1913.

The period of meditation I mentioned above had come to an end. 1913–14 were the golden years of Villon's graphic work, however rich a harvest it may have produced in other periods of his life. After following the various phases of Cubism, simultaneously with the birth of Synthetic Cubism he struck out on his own and created Impressionist Cubism. In fifteen engravings, of which twelve are truly masterly achievements, he reached an unequaled peak of perfection. Drypoint and etching were the only media he employed.

Villon's Cubism is always in close contact with man and reality. It displays an extraordinary conception of planes, a play of light and shade achieved with triangular or lozenge-shaped facets that recall the sparkle of a diamond in the sun. The result is a glistening iridescence that is quite unique, enhanced by the velvety blacks that only the drypoint can produce. Unlike the works of other Cubist engravers, Villon's give the impression of being the only ones done by a painter. It is interesting to note that, whereas he had formerly executed his engravings after drawn sketches, he did these after paintings.

It is also important to stress the fact that, though he was the initiator of the Golden Section Exhibition and even responsible for its title, Villon never lost sight of humanity and the need for artistic creation. Although he was intensely interested in discussing artistic problems and snatched at every pretext to do so in his studio at Puteaux, which was a meeting place for his brothers Marcel Duchamp and Raymond Duchamp-Villon, and his friends Albert Gleizes, Jean Metzinger, Roger de La Fresnaye, Francis Picabia, Frank Kupka, André Mare, Paul Fort, Guillaume Apollinaire, Ribemont-

Dessaignes and Jean Cocteau. But he was far from being a cool theoretician and always kept his feet on the ground. He remained loyal to Cubist discipline but sought his inspiration in nature, not copying it slavishly but making every painting or engraving a creative act. As he said himself, "Total abstraction is not for me. I love life and the visible world far too well for that."

Yvonne Duchamp, one of the artist's sisters, was the model for this work. We see her in three-quarter profile seated in an armchair, reading a book. Her serious face is illuminated by the lamp on her right. There were two states of this plate, the first printed in eleven copies, the second in twenty-three. It is a splendid specimen of this second state that is reproduced here.

Yvonne D. from the Side, 1913.
Drypoint, 55 × 41.2 cm. Second state. No. 8/23.
Bibliography: Auberty and Pérussaux 194.
Private Collection.

P./143

73

This print is considered Villon's masterpiece. It is not only the most important of his Cubist engravings but also of his entire graphic *œuvre*, which comprises over seven hundred sheets. Like the portrait of his sister Yvonne, it was executed in 1913.

In the *Great Testament* he compiled for the catalogue of the show of his graphic work in the French National Library in 1959, Villon wrote: ". . . My first color prints were images and therefore could adorn a wall, but engraving in black and white is better suited to express an art which, like all arts, probes man's heart and conscience. . . . There is only one art that propounds signs which are the equivalent of objects, combining abstraction and reality—is anything more abstract than a line, a stroke, a drawing made of lines, of crisscross strokes?—and that art is engraving. . ., the art found in caves and on copperplates. . . ."

These thoughts, which the artist wrote down towards the end of his life, were those he had put into practise in 1910 when he abandoned color aquatint for the magical, fantastic, fascinating effects achieved in black and white with simple strokes, hatchings and cross-hatchings made by a steel point on a copperplate. The reproduction on the opposite page, no matter how fine it may be, cannot render the velvety, mat, deep blacks produced with the drypoint, particularly on proofs pulled before steel-plating. One must see this print and the preceding one "in the original" to grasp fully what Villon aimed at and discover what the word "fascination" really means.

Villon devoted a lot of study to the theme of *The Laid Table*. Dora Vallier has described four preliminary drawings for the engraving, all dated 1912, and two paintings dated 1913. The drawing shows us how the artist developed his idea, of which the engraving represents the final stage.

On a rectangular rustic table with heavy turned legs a cloth is spread; on the cloth we see a haphazard array of dishes, plates, glasses, bottles, decanters, fruits; at the upper left are the rounded backs of two chairs. Everything on the table is depicted in curves, in a myriad of crescent shapes. There are no straight lines. These latter are used solely for the table itself and for the setting that frames this still life, which sparkles with an amazing liveliness.

This print was exhibited for the first time at the Salon d'Automne of 1913. Thirty signed and numbered copies of the first state, before steel-plating, were printed in addition to a few proofs. The artist signed and authenticated the same number of copies of the second state, which were printed after the plate had been cut down and steel-plated.

The Laid Table, 1913.
Drypoint, 28.6 × 38.6 cm. First state. No. 4/30.
Bibliography: Auberty and Pérussaux 196.
Collection Marcel Lecomte, Paris.

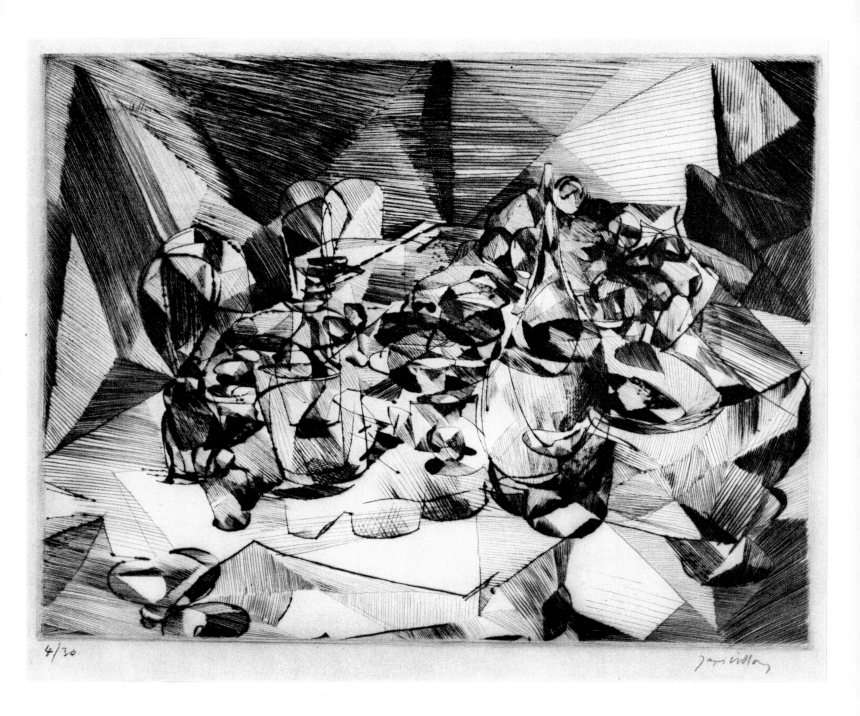

4/30

Jacques Villon

This is one of Vlaminck's finest woodcuts. The subject is the port of Martigues and the artist engraved the block with a gouge in about 1907. The woodcuts executed by Vlaminck and Derain during the years when they were close friends are extremely interesting because they display the same ebullient temperament we find in the explosive paintings of their Fauve period. These vigorous, forceful woodcuts were violent reactions against the academic insipidity that characterized the degenerate productions of most wood engravers of that day.

In 1901 Bernheim-Jeune organized a show of Van Gogh's work which had consequences of the first importance. When Vlaminck and Derain were viewing the show the latter met Matisse and introduced him to his friend. More important still, Vlaminck and Derain were dumbfounded by Van Gogh's work, which they had never seen before. It was a revelation. Such was Vlaminck's enthusiasm for the Dutch artist that in the train, on his way back to Chatou, he shouted at the top of his voice: "I love Van Gogh more than my own father!" You can imagine the station-master's amazement.

This enthusiasm is reflected in his woodcuts, *Martigues Harbor, The Bridge at Chatou* and *Bougival,* notably in the stormy skies with the clouds spiraling round the exploding sun. These woodcuts were purchased by Henry Kahnweiler, a dealer who was one of Picasso's friends.

Kahnweiler made his mark when still a young man not only as a picture dealer but also as an outstanding publisher. He brought out his first book, *L'Enchanteur pourrissant,* in 1909. It was the first book by Guillaume Apollinaire and the first illustrated by Derain, who did thirty-two woodcuts for it. About the same time Kahnweiler published some woodcuts by Vlaminck, including those mentioned above. Since he was a German his property was seized when war broke out in 1914. It was only freed in 1923 and the works that had been sequestrated were sold by auction at the Hôtel Drouot. At the sale Vlaminck's woodcuts were bought by a print dealer named Maurice Le Garrec.

In 1956 Le Garrec's grandson, Jean-Claude Romand, decided to hold an exhibition of Vlaminck's work in his gallery on the Rue du Four. He went to see the artist, who was living at Rueil-la-Gadelière, and showed him the prints he planned to show. Among them were the famous woodcuts Vlaminck had not laid eyes on for over forty years. "The deuce! How fine they are!" he exclaimed. He was so enthusiastic that he put his signature to the trial proofs, which he had left unsigned. This explains how it is that the definitive prints bear his old signature and the trial proofs his most recent one, for he died two years later.

Martigues Harbor, c. 1907.
Woodcut, 33.9 × 41.5 cm, No. 54.
Bibliography: Catalogue of the Berne Exhibition, 1961, No. 20.
Private Collection.

N: 54   Vlaminck

In addition to woodcuts Vlaminck produced lithographs in color and in black and white. Another medium he used was etching. *The Oise at Sergy after the Storm* may well be called his masterpiece in this latter technique.

For this splendid print the artist did the drawing directly on to the copperplate exclusively with a brush. The handling of the landscape displays all the painter's vigorous, energetic temperament. The touches of black over the various tones of gray achieve a breathtaking three-dimensional effect and together with the reflection of trees and clouds on the surface of the water make this print a truly great work. The storm has just blown over; the atmosphere freed from the slightest trace of dust or mist has a crystal clarity that the artist has rendered miraculously on the copperplate.

A detailed scrutiny of this print leads one to conclude that Vlaminck employed the sugar process, which produces a ground similar to that of the aquatint. But there is also the possibility that the sheet had to be run twice through the press, the second time for the touches of black. This could have been done either with a different copperplate or after working over the same one. However, the print shows no sign of registering. According to Jacques Frapier, the publisher's son, the impression was carried out by Delâtre.

The engraving was executed by Vlaminck in 1923 and published in May 1924 in an album entitled *Maîtres et Petits Maîtres d'Aujourd'hui*. It went through two states that differ only in that the second has the artist's signature engraved on the plate. The first state consisted of twenty-five copies for the *de luxe* albums; the second of twenty-five for the double set of *de luxe* albums and one hundred for the standard albums. All the prints were signed and numbered by the artist and the plate was scored after the printing.

Vlaminck considered this one of his finest engravings—an opinion shared by a great many people.

The Oise at Sergy, 1923.
Aquatint, 23.9 × 31.7 cm. Second state. No. 15/100.
Bibliography: Catalogue of the Berne Exhibition, 1961, No. 30.
Private Collection, formerly Templier Collection.

15/100

The brilliant illustrator of Alphonse Daudet's *Tartarin de Tarascon*—his one hundred and seven lithographs made it one of the finest illustrated books published in the twentieth century—used to say that the work was closer in spirit to Marseilles than to Tarascon. He had reached that conclusion after traveling all the way to Tarascon to breathe in the atmosphere of the town in which the scene was laid.

Raoul Dufy was born at Le Havre and, like Marquet, felt the pull of seaports, particularly Marseilles, which pleased him for its southern liveliness and the gaiety of its population. He painted it as early as 1908 on a canvas that displays a very fine composition of masts and hulls. In 1925, the year in which this lithograph was executed, he painted a view of the harbor with the very same background as we see here. The painting, now in the Brussels Museum, is taller than it is broad. The foreground represents the balcony of the painter's bedroom, so we can say with certainty that in the print he has depicted the view of the harbor as he saw it from his window there. The buildings, the old transporter bridge later destroyed by the Germans, the row of boats on the right, and the tugboat at the quayside on the left are the same as in the painting. But the bottom quarter of the latter shows us the splendid wrought ironwork of the balcony and above it the pedestrian and horse traffic on the quay below. In the lithograph railing and quay have disappeared to make room for a charming mythological composition, typical of Dufy, comprising dolphins, bathers and sea-horses. Some of the latter pull a shell-shaped chariot with a blonde Venus rising from the foam. The pencil that served Dufy as a magic wand has changed the cab-horses of the painting into sea-horses frolicking among the waves.

This lithograph formed part of a portfolio that was published in thirty-three copies in 1925 and was received with the utmost indifference. It contained six lithographs, of which four were in black and white and two in color—this one and *Boats* produced overleaf. The cardboard cover was adorned with a seventh, smaller lithograph. Today it is practically impossible to lay hands on the portfolio: the edition was extremely limited for a start and most of the plates have been sold separately. The titles of the four in black and white are *The Dive, Six Bathers, Fishes* and *Regatta*.

This extremely fine print displays all the painter's highly colored imagination. It is imbued with an airy, joyful atmosphere that breathes love of life; it throbs with the gaiety of Raoul Dufy's world.

Marseilles Harbor, 1925.
Lithograph in color, 33 × 44.2 cm, No. 10/33.
Published by Editions de l'Etoile.
Private Collection.

This splendid lithograph, which, like the preceding one, was comprised in the portfolio entitled *The Sea*, constitutes a Dufy festival all by itself. The artist has treated it as he treated his watercolors, composing with a freedom that was one of his most typical traits a fantastic, brightly colored flotilla ranging from one of the three-masters he loved so well, through a paddle steamer and a yacht dressed overall, to a little racing cutter. There is even a heavy cruiser firing a broadside. Only his famous little black freighter is missing in this squadron that represents the pleasure of painting : it had not been invented yet.

Blue is the dominant color in this print. It is a color Dufy was particularly attracted to. For those who knew him it recalls his eyes, which were an extraordinary turquoise blue. Dufy was fond of repeating that blue was the only color that kept its own personality in all its shades. "Take any other color," he would say, "for instance red. Well, if it is dark it becomes brown; if it is diluted with white it becomes pink. In either case it is no longer red but another color. As for yellow, it gets black in the shadows and loses its brightness in the highlights. Blue alone, in every shade, dark or light, navy or sky, is always a distinct color—blue."

Dufy used to tell the story of how one day, at the height of Cubism, he saw a little girl in a red dress playing on the beach. All of a sudden the little girl and her red dress separated. Was it an optical illusion or had the child simply taken off her dress to go into the water and flung it on the back of a chair or on a spade stuck into the sand ? For Dufy it was a revelation. From then on color no longer kept to line; it overflowed the line; it won its freedom, lived its own life; it was no longer a prisoner; it lived and, he said, became joy because it danced.

Dufy was, indeed, the painter of joy and joy was as necessary to him as the air he breathed. Here is a little story—one of many—to prove this, and also to prove his passion for music and for the sea. In 1950, after undergoing cortisone treatment in Boston for his rheumatism, he rented a ranch in Arizona but was soon bored by the life he led there. Boredom was something quite unknown to Dufy : to drive it away he started painting marine scenes in fresco on the walls of the house. In the new climate he created with his waves, boats and bathers, and "with Debussy's *The Sea* on my gramophone, I recovered my joy, all my joy."

Boats, 1925.
Color lithograph, 35.2 × 47.3 cm, No. 33/33.
Published by Editions de l'Etoile.
Private Collection.

83

Jean-Emile Laboureur, "the prince of engravers," occupies an important place in the history of French engraving. He was only nineteen years old when he started to make prints and profited by advice from Toulouse-Lautrec and that great wood engraver Auguste Lepère. It was he who in 1920 initiated Dunoyer de Segonzac in etching and was, indeed, his sole teacher. Edouard Goerg said he owed it to Laboureur that he kept on engraving and took up etching on his advice. It is interesting to note that though Laboureur was the leading French engraver of the first half of the century, he did not force either Segonzac or Goerg to follow in his footsteps and keep to line engraving: his instinct told him what their proper sphere would be. Laboureur was the founder of the Society of Independent Painter-Engravers and all his life long fostered print making with an energy that gave it a new span of life.

Laboureur was an engraver in the broadest sense of the term. Besides line engraving, in which he excelled, he employed many other media: woodcut —he was born at Nantes and knew an industrialist called Lotz-Brissonneau, who must have introduced him to Lepère—, etching, drypoint, soft-ground, aquatint and lithography. It was Toulouse-Lautrec who initiated him in this last technique. He invited Laboureur to visit him in Ancourt's workshop, where he used to spend the morning executing lithographs, and learn what he called the "tek-nik" of drawing on stone. And it was under Lautrec's supervision that Laboureur did his first lithograph. In thirty-two years it was followed by eighty others, but he found his three hundred and eighty woodcuts a more congenial occupation. It is interesting to note that in one year, 1929, he gave up both media entirely and thereafter devoted himself to etching and line engraving, until 1939, when he left unfinished his last copperplates.

The Shooting Gallery was engraved in 1920. It immediately met with success and was reproduced in *L'Amour de l'Art* in August of that year. This line engraving passed through four states. Six proofs were pulled of the first, eight of the second, seven of the third. The fourth, definitive state was printed in eighty-five copies plus a certain number of artist's proofs. It counts, with *The News-stand* (1920), *Laundresses* (1922), *Balcony on the Sea* (1923) and *The Entomologist* (1923), among Laboureur's masterpieces and is perhaps the greatest of them all. Two years before he had executed a woodcut with the same title (Loyer 715-7), in which one sees two soldiers in forage caps standing at a fair-ground shooting gallery. The woman in charge stands on the left-hand side. There is the same fringed pelmet at the top and the same curtain on the left. This means that for the print reproduced here Laboureur took his cue from its predecessor, but in 1920 the two men had naturally become civilians.

The Shooting Gallery, 1920.
Line engraving, 26.9 × 22.5 cm. Fourth state, artist's proof.
Bibliography: L. Godefroy 191.
Private Collection.

Laboureur   éj. d'artiste

When Frélaut died in 1954, Dunoyer de Segonzac wrote the following paragraph on the flyleaf of my copy of the delightful set of etchings entitled *Villages*, which Frélaut had engraved twenty years before for the "5/20" (five engravers, twenty art lovers).

"My friend Jean Frélaut was one of the very few contemporary artists who deserve to be called 'saints.' His work is the mirror reflection of his soul. It is the result of pious meditation on nature and on life. He will always be one of the greatest poets of Brittany, the land of his birth, and of the noble, grave Armorican countryside where he found his inspiration."

There could be no better definition of Frélaut. He was a poet-engraver and Brittany was the land he loved best. It was there that he did most of his landscapes, which are drawn with a charm that no contemporary engraver has equaled. Their artless candor rests on a skill which is worthy of Rembrandt himself but is concealed by the poetry that emanates from these admirable little prints; they are so delicately and minutely limned that despite their small size they manage to suggest broad horizons. His little figures, which recall those Van Ostade engraved in the seventeenth century, breathe grace and kindliness and bear witness to Frélaut's great love for the humble Breton peasant folk.

Etchings like *Snow* (1921), the admirable *Winter Landscape* (1928), the delightful *Little Valley* (1932) or *Rural Wedding* (1933–7) are splendid examples of that medium. But Frélaut's masterpiece is this *Winter Night*. The moon shines through the leafless branches, casting a magic light over the magnificent landscape. Its subtle reverberation on the snow, the feather-light shadows of the trees and the nocturnal mystery it creates are rendered with amazing mastery. That is what makes this print an outstanding example of twentieth-century engrav-

ing. It is a cogent illustration of Frélaut's own saying : "Painting has color, but engraving has light." Then there is the vast range of blacks—the velvety black of the sky, the deeper black of the trees—and the impalpable grays of the shadows. This is something one simply cannot forget. And lastly, there is the wolf—just to remind us what a magnificent engraver of animals Frélaut was and of his splendid illustrations for *The Fables* of La Fontaine.

Frélaut first engraved the copperplate in 1933 for *January*, one of a set of *The Months of the Year* printed in twelve copies. In 1941 he worked over the plate in depth and, after a number of trial proofs of which one is reproduced here, pulled ten signed prints. After that the plate was destroyed.

It was Frélaut's custom to make sketches and delightful little watercolors directly from nature and engrave his plates after them in the studio. He had his own hand press and printed the proofs himself. He was not only a great artist but also a skilled craftsman.

Winter Night, 1941.
Etching, 14.8 × 19.9 cm. Proof on antique green paper.
Bibliography: Supplement to Delteil, P. Cailler 410 (not yet published).
Private Collection.

André Derain produced almost five hundred and fifty prints including a few line engravings, about a hundred etchings and drypoints and some one hundred and fifty lithographs. But woodcuts in color and in black and white account for more than half the total.

In 1906, after trying his hand at a few etchings, Derain took up wood engraving at Chatou together with his friend Vlaminck. But it was not till 1940 that he became interested in color woodcuts. He did so with a view to illustrating Albert Skira's edition of the *Pantagruel* of Rabelais, one of the finest books published in this century. It contains a hundred and twenty-eight color woodcuts, chapter headings and tailpieces, all engraved by Derain himself and printed by Lacourière.

Jacques Frélaut told me about the production of this book, on which five journeymen printers worked for three years under Derain's supervision. *Bunch of Flowers in a Vase*, the first woodcut executed for the book, was ultimately discarded.

Derain started work on the block with the idea of simply making an experiment; then he and Frélaut used it to "sample" the colors. The result was a masterpiece. The harmonious effect produced by the composition of the vase, the choice of colors, the unpolished workmanship that Derain insisted on because for his illustrations of Rabelais he wanted a type of engraving close to that used for printing *tarot* cards in the fifteenth century, make this print a delightful work.

The technique differs from that generally employed, which involves as many blocks as there are colors. Derain wanted to use a single block and run it through the press only once. So he had to cut out his design with a gouge and isolate the colors with deep furrows in order to prevent their overlapping. Each area thus separated was hand-painted with the color he had chosen, and the process was repeated for each single print.

The book was published in an edition of two hundred and sixty-five copies. It took three years to produce because there were more than thirty-five thousand prints, each of which had to be done by hand. The illustrations can be divided into two sorts, one finer than the other. In a first batch of prints the color showed the brush strokes. That did not displease Derain but the publisher preferred flat, uniform patches of color. So there is not a trace of the brush in the remainder of the edition. After the first woodcut was printed the artist realized that the white had to be toned down, so he added a very pale watercolor. The result was perfect harmony.

Bunch of Flowers in a Vase, 1940.
Color woodcut, 27.8 × 17.2 cm. No. 61/100.
Published by A. Skira.
Galerie Sources, Paris.

45/100

Picasso was eighteen years old when, in 1899, he first took in hand a small copperplate and engraved a picador. Only one proof of the print is still extant and, though invaluable from a historical point of view, offers little artistic interest.

In 1904 he did his second engraving—*The Frugal Meal*—one of his masterpieces and at the same time one of the outstanding examples of twentieth-century engraving. This capital work affords further proof that for a painter-engraver of genius engraving is, and must remain, a secondary activity. What little technical skill Picasso had learnt from the painter Ricardo Canale, an old friend from the days of the "Quatre Gats," when they lived in the Bateau Lavoir at Montmartre sufficed for the execution of this masterwork.

In those days Picasso was too poor to buy a brand new copperplate of such large size, so he made do with a zinc plate on which another artist had already engraved a landscape. He did two states of the etching, after which some thirty splendid prints were pulled by Delâtre. Despite the efforts of the dealer Sagot, they were a total failure.

In 1913 Ambroise Vollard bought from Picasso all the zinc and copperplates he had engraved in 1904 and 1905. He had them steel-plated with the idea of printing a large edition—two hundred and eighty sets entitled *Saltimbanques*. Nine years had passed since the plates were engraved; they had all become oxidized, especially those in zinc, and steel-plating only accentuated this defect. It brought out others too, for the design of the original landscape can be seen on the later prints of *The Frugal Meal*, which were pulled after that process had been applied. The Vollard edition, which was printed by Fort, can be recognized by this particular, as well as by their pale tone, lacking in contrast and relief, and far inferior to that of the Delâtre impression. Vollard himself was the first

to realize this and was extremely anxious to obtain possession of the proof of *The Frugal Meal* that Picasso had given André Salmon in 1904.

Before tackling the plate Picasso did a preliminary drawing, which was exhibited (No. 12) in the Petit Salon in November 1966. He used the same drawing for the painting put on show in Paris among the *Masterpieces of the Swiss Collections* (No. 239) in 1967. The composition is identical in the drawing and the painting. The man is on the right, his head seen in profile but bare and bent, his eyes closed. Only one of his hands and one of the woman's are visible. One misses the magnificent rhythm of the four hands—such a striking feature of the etching—with their purposely elongated fingers, the man's turned towards the right, the woman's towards the left, which imprison the woman in her unhappy fate and stress the dramatic conditions in which the blind man and his companion, like all the suffering humanity of Picasso's blue period, lived.

It is a splendid proof of the 1904 printing that is reproduced here. Picasso countersigned it in 1949.

The Frugal Meal, 1904.
Etching on zinc, 46.3 × 37.7 cm. Second state before steel-plating.
Bibliography: B. Geiser, Vol. I, No. 2 A.
Private Collection.

"The blind Minotaur passes through a harbor at night, guided by a child with large, clear-seeing eyes, and hopelessly raises the ghost of his dead gaze towards the starry sky. On the left of the engraving a fisherman stands by a lighted fire; on the right some sardines sparkle in a net. . . ."

Jacques Prévert, Spectacle (N.R.F.)

This print, which has been greatly admired by Prévert and Eluard, is one of the finest of the set of a hundred plates known as the *Vollard Series* because it was the dealer Ambroise Vollard who sent Picasso the copperplates in 1930 or thereabouts and told him to engrave them as he liked. The series was executed between 1930 and 1937 and comprises forty-six prints on the theme of the *Sculptor's Studio* and fifteen on the *Minotaur*. Of these latter the four last, which were engraved towards the end of 1934, represent *The Blind Minotaur*.

The Minotaur theme was one of those that had interested Picasso ever since 1927, when he painted *Minotaur and Sleeping Woman*. Tériade and Skira had founded a review whose title, *Minotaure*, seems to have been suggested by André Masson. The cover of the first issue (May 25, 1933) was designed by Picasso. This launched him on a new trail that led to a great quantity of drawings, gouaches and, in particular, prints.

The fire mentioned by Prévert lights up all the figures and one is amazed at the force and delicacy with which it brings out every slightest detail of the Minotaur's muscular frame and magnificent head. The same fire lights up the pure Grecian profile of the girl who holds the dove, a symbol of which Picasso is so fond. It lights up the faces of the awestruck fishermen, who are busying themselves about a boat that rests on an even keel. It also lights up the youth one finds in so many of Picasso's works pondering on life's great themes. Here brute force subdued; there, the mystery of a woman's naked body; there again, the misery of the human condition. The whole is treated in a classical, almost Ingresque manner but with an extraordinary painterly force.

In the print reproduced here Picasso employed three techniques—aquatint, etching and line engraving. With all a painter's skill he has eluded the shoals of academic classicism thanks to the dazzling light, which is an element of capital importance in a work where all the whites are obtained with burnisher and scraper. Then, as if displeased by the excessive perfection of his drawing, he took a burin to simplify the forms. The retouches with the burin stress the boy's profile, his hands, his arms, his trousers. They do the same for the Minotaur's right hand that rests on the girl's shoulder. Finally, the artist did not hesitate to use etching for the purpose of rendering and intensifying the amazement of the two fishermen, which the burnisher could not have expressed with sufficient vigor.

The Blind Minotaur, 1934.
Aquatint treated as a mezzotint, 24.7 × 34.7 cm.
Published first by A. Vollard, later by H.-M. Petiet.
Bibliography: B. Geiser, Vol. II, No. 437.
Private Collection.

This is the finest of the set of one hundred prints published by Vollard and, as in the preceding one, the lighting is of capital importance. The artist's genius succeeds in giving us the impression that the early morning sun of the Mediterranean is streaming into the room through the narrow window, dispersing the shades of night. This wondrous light floods the entire scene with Dionysian joy. It casts a diagonal across the room dividing it into two parts, one dark, one light. But the "dark" portion is no less marvelous than the "light" one. The shades of gray on the woman's face, on the walls and on the ceiling have a subtlety seldom equaled and it is largely to them that this masterwork owes its fascination. Their delicate beauty give the measure of the painterly quality one admires in so many of Picasso's engravings.

Every detail of this print is splendid. In addition to the light, we must admire the extraordinary foreshortening of the sleeping woman's relaxed body, the classical profile of the faun, his attitude of ardent desire for the woman, and the setting which the artist has drawn so ably with brush and scraper. With a brush, because one of the techniques he employed for this plate is sugar engraving. It was in 1935 that the master printer Lacourière initiated Picasso in the sugar process, for which the paintbrush is the customary tool. The painter at once adopted what for him was a new medium, mastered it rapidly, and employed it with amazing virtuosity. He used it, notably, in 1937 in the thirty-two engravings for his Buffon, which, as Sabartès, who saw Picasso at work, tells us, were "dashed off" at the rate of at least one a day. He used it too for the twenty-seven engravings of his prestigious *Tauromachy* in 1959.

Faun Uncovering a Woman went through four states and was finished on June 12, 1936. In the following year Picasso finished all the plates of the series and Vollard had them printed by Lacourière. The edition comprised close on three hundred copies on fine Montval paper, plus three on vellum. Only the latter were signed at the time. After Ambroise Vollard's death in 1939 two leading Paris dealers bought the prints from his brother Lucien. One acquired the three portraits of Vollard, the other the remaining ninety-nine. Both had Picasso sign their prints on various occasions for many of them were still unsigned.

The copperplates for the set were scored in 1956.

Faun Uncovering a Woman, 1936.
Aquatint and line engraving, 31.5 × 41.7 cm.
Published first by A. Vollard, later by H.-M. Petiet.
Bibliography: B. Geiser, Vol. III (not yet published).
Private Collection.

So many of Picasso's engravings are masterpieces that it is no easy matter to establish a classification. But this print, which, like all the others, should be examined in the original, is an extraordinary work and must be placed in the first flight because of its monumental size, its composition, its subject, and what Robert Nanteuil called its "handling." This latter recalls Rodolphe Bresdin's prints, of which Picasso is a collector. There is also a historical factor, namely the premonition of future threats to humanity : indeed, some people see it as a prefiguration of *Guernica*. However that may be, in my eyes *Minotauromachy* shares with *The Dove* (see p. 99, Mourlot 141) pride of place among Picasso's engravings; it is certainly the most sought after of them all. Unfortunately it has become extremely rare. This is because the huge copperplate—the largest of all Picasso's engravings on metal—was executed, probably at his home, Boisgeloup Castle, in 1935 and only printed in some thirty copies, which he did not authenticate. Henri Petiet told me that the lack of numbering was due to the fact that Picasso, who is an extremely scrupulous artist, could not recall the exact order in which the first prints were pulled; so, rather than make a mistake, he preferred to omit all authentication of those that followed. On the copy reproduced here, which Madame Louise Leiris so very kindly lent me, one can read the indication in the artist's own hand that the edition comprised thirty copies. There were also some state and artist's proofs, which Picasso presented to his closest friends and to the magnificent Sabartès Collection of Picasso engravings in the Barrio Gotico in Barcelona.

This print is the most important of all those of the Minotaur suite. The dramatic scene is limned in a moment of what one feels is an unstable equilibrium. The Minotaur's brute force is still held in check and has not yet been unleashed. But we realize its menace. Facing it are only a handful of peaceable, fragile figures—two delicate blond young girls at the window with two doves, a man who resembles St. John the Baptist, a little girl with a bunch of flowers and a candle, a female bullfighter in a faint, and a weak little horse whose entrails are pouring out of its gored belly. It is interesting to note that Picasso has never represented the Minotaur in the act of brutalizing, wounding or killing. He has always shown him amorous, timid, invalid or even dying. Here the monster is more threatening, but he fears the candlelight and his gesture dispels the atmosphere of terror, leaving simply an anxiety that only the horse, which is already wounded, and the man climbing up the ladder to escape seem to feel.

In Picasso's eyes the myth of the Minotaur is often linked with that of the bull and the bullfighter. This astonishing print affords one more proof of that.

Minotauromachy, 1935.
Etching, 50 × 69.5 cm. One of the 30 prints.
Bibliography: B. Geiser, Vol. III (not yet published).
Collection Louise Leiris, Paris.

Une des Vinitas épreuves d'essai   Picasso 13

This is the finest of all Picasso's lithographs. In the opinion of so great an expert as Fernand Mourlot, it is one of the finest lithographs ever produced. Every time one sees it one feels the same intense emotion.

From the technical viewpoint, it is the most perfect work ever achieved with lithographic ink applied as a wash. The subtle tones of the bird's plumage produce the same delicate effect as its downy feathers do in real life. From the artistic viewpoint, this dove radiates an extraordinary vitality : one feels it palpitate with innocence and peace. One is amazed by the posture of the head : the slight inclination from front to back and towards the spectator makes it dazzlingly clear how well the artist knows and loves the bird, whose eye he has rendered so perfectly. Picasso has reverted to the theme of the dove again and again. The messenger of peace appears, chiefly in his engravings, either alone or as a symbolic element of the composition. The plate for the print reproduced here was executed on January 9, 1949, for stereotyping in thousands of copies as a poster for the Peace Congress held in April of that year.

For the purpose Picasso used a zinc plate, which is handier than a heavy lithographic stone, and drew his design with a paintbrush dipped in lithographic ink, which he diluted with kerosene for the areas where he wanted to obtain a delicate shaded white. This brings us back to what happens when a painter takes up print making. Sabartès has explained that when Picasso went to the Mourlot brothers' workshop on November 2, 1945, he did so no doubt in order to become more familiar with lithography; in fact, from 1919 to 1945 he had produced only twenty-seven works in that medium. But from the very start he showed that he had technical ideas of his own, which had nothing in common with the traditions of the trade. Mourlot was sufficiently open-minded to understand him and, instead of violently countering those ideas and forbidding Picasso access to his workshop, as so many printers do with lesser artists, he gave him the free run of it and let him absorb its atmosphere. Picasso conceived a real passion for that atmosphere and for the contact with printers, stones, ink and presses. The result was that for four long years—interspersed, needless to say, with frequent intervals—he executed lithographs at Mourlot's, arriving at nine in the morning and only leaving at eight in the evening. He would dig into his pockets for his own personal tools, a little penknife, another shaped like a sickle, a scrap of emery paper, his paintbrushes, even glue—"for reserving the whites," as he explained to a dumbfounded Mourlot.

Five artist's proofs and fifty signed and numbered copies were printed on Arches paper from the magnificent plate. After that printing it was erased.

The Dove, 1949.
Lithograph on zinc, 54.5 × 70 cm. Trial print.
Published by Galerie Leiris.
Bibliography: Mourlot, Vol. I, No. 141.
Collection Mourlot Bros., Paris.

A los toros ! Sabartès tells us that when he was still a small boy Picasso used to go to the bullfight, holding his father's hand. All his life he has been obsessed by the bull, which he has studied thoroughly and portrayed more times than one can count. To render the beast's postures he has employed all the techniques used in engraving, choosing sugar aquatint for his masterly illustrations of Pepe Illo's *Tauromaquia, o Arte de Torear.* But it is in linocuts that he has shown us what he feels as an *aficionado,* a connoisseur of the bull ring. And in this medium too masterpieces have blossomed under his hand.

Picasso executed his first linocut in 1939. It was entitled *The Young Pigeon* and was only published in black and white in 1957. The next one dates from 1958. It is the impressive *Bust of a Girl after the Younger Cranach* in six colors reproduced in the section of this book devoted to the definition of engraving techniques (p. 19). With this important work Picasso began the series of over one hundred and fifty linocuts that he executed within a very few years. Until then the inert medium had lain virtually dormant and, despite the efforts of Matisse and other artists, had never produced a work of the first importance. Picasso took it up and used if for genuine masterpieces. He became passionately interested in the new technique, exploring its potentialities, renovating, innovating, and making a decisive contribution to its development.

Till then the flabbiness of the linoleum, which, as Lorjou says, offers no resistance to the cutting tool, condamned the medium to be used exclusively for the production of lifeless, academic works. One has only to glance at this print to realize Picasso's creative force. He has ravished the material and subjected it to his will, giving it an amazing vitality and vigor. In his hands flabbiness has given way to violence.

The action has an extraordinary intensity, the furious gesture bursts with truth, the encounter of man and beast is caught at its culminating point, and the dramatic power is stressed by the radiating streaks, whose clever arrangement is perhaps the most unusual feature of the work and gives it strength while clothing it in light.

This linocut in three colors was printed, like virtually all those Picasso produced, by Arnera at Vallauris in fifty copies and a few artist's proofs. It is the last engraving by Picasso reproduced in this book for, unfortunately, one must stop somewhere. But the selection shown here bears witness to the genius of an artist who, at eighty-seven years of age, has just finished engraving three hundred and forty-seven copper plates in six months and a half, with unheard-of gusto and tireless ardor. That is a feat no other artist has ever performed in the six centuries since engraving was invented— not even the most prolific in the first flush of youth.

Banderillas, 1959.
Linocut in three colors, 53 × 64 cm.
Published by Galerie Leiris.
Bibliography: Catalogue Galerie Leiris 1960, No. 37; Catalogue Berggruen 1964, No. 309.
Collection Louise Leiris, Paris.

Braque, unlike Toulouse-Lautrec, gave color precedence over line in his lithographs. Proof of this is the fact that of the one hundred and eighty lithographs he produced one hundred and forty-eight are in color. Fernand Mourlot says that even where, as in *Helios*, the linework is important he made several experiments for the blue because he wanted to obtain four different shades and that demanded four simultaneous printings. Braque also studied several colors for the frame of this lithograph. In the end he selected four tints, which made it necessary to run the same sheet of paper four times through the press. In view of the large number of impressions and of superimposed colors the black and white stone—in this case the design—had to be printed last. This print involved nine runs through the press.

Braque executed his first lithograph in 1921; his second, which was merely the cover for a catalogue, in 1928; his third, entitled *Athenaeum*, in 1932; his fourth, *Phaeton*, in 1945. So he really only took up that medium after World War II, when he was already sixty-three years old. This means that his lithographs belong to the third period of his graphic *œuvre*.

It may be recalled that his first period (1908–12) was Cubist. It consists of etchings, some of them very close to Picasso's. His second period (1921–34) was overshadowed by Hesiod's *Theogony*, which Vollard asked him to illustrate in 1931. Braque was fascinated by the poetic nomenclature of the divinities of Greek mythology and executed sixteen impressive etchings in a curvilinear style interspersed with Greek characters, which interested him for their ideographical content. That masterwork was published by Maeght in 1954 with four additional etchings.

In 1946 Braque worked on the Helios theme in Mourlot's workshop. He was put in mind of his engravings for Hesiod's *Theogony* and the lithograph, *Athenaeum*, which that poem had inspired. He became passionately interested in the theme, which provided the basis for five lithographs in addition to a closely related woodcut entitled *Persephone*. The artist started by drawing his subject in ink on lithographic paper. The design was transferred to the stone and printed in white on a ground prepared with a zinc plate (Mourlot 9). The same design also exists on a different ground (M. 10). Next, printed in black, it served for the lithograph reproduced here, of which there were seventy-five numbered copies plus a few proofs. It was used a fourth time for a lithograph in six colors on a mauve ground (M. 12), and lastly for the cover of *Braque's Sketchbooks* (M. 13).

This sumptuous work, in which the Sun god, radiating a dazzling light, passes through the shades of Night in his chariot, is one of the great painter-engraver's most sought-after lithographs.

Helios, 1946.
Lithograph in nine colors, 50.5 × 42 cm. Trial print.
Bibliography: Mourlot 11.
Collection Mourlot Bros., Paris.

This lithograph in six colors—one of the most famous executed by Braque—dates from 1947. The subject was one of those that concerned him most during that period. He had already done two lithographs, *Teapot and Apples* (Mourlot 6) in seven colors and *Teapot on a Gray Ground* (M. 8) in five colors, the year before. The oil painting of 1948, *Teapot and Lemon*, with areas of thick impasto, is directly derived from the lithograph of 1947. Lastly, in 1949, another important lithograph, similarly entitled *Teapot and Lemons* (M. 21), brought to a close the teapot series, of which the last-named work and the one reproduced here are the finest.

Braque, as we have already seen, became passionately interested in lithography in 1945 as a result of his meeting with Fernand Mourlot. Incidentally, in that same year Picasso also continued his lithographic production—already more extensive than Braque's—with great assiduity in the Mourlots' workshop. It is interesting to observe the parallel development of the two great painters' artistic activity : together they had invented Cubism and they both became intensely interested in lithography at the same time. Braque has told us how he was tempted by that medium and how "I tried to treat it in a new way. Instead of following tradition and doing merely a sort of heightened drawing, I did what almost amounted to painting." It must be said, however, that, were it not for the skill and personality of Fernand Mourlot, the capability of the team he formed, and the peculiar atmosphere that he and his brothers created in their workshop, Picasso would never have spent long days there for months on end to produce so many masterworks, nor would Braque and Chagall—to mention only two artists among many—have done so many lithographs there in 1947.

Braque was a wonderful painter of still lifes and chose the subjects of his lithographs with great simplicity. The simplicity of the subject matter enabled him to concentrate his researches and adopt a procedure that transcends the notion of the object. As he said himself in a talk with Richardson, quoted in the *Catalogue of Braque's Graphic Œuvre* (B.N. 1960), at the time he was doing his famous *Birds* : "For me objects only exist in so far as there is a relationship between them or between them and myself. When one achieves this harmony one attains a sort of intellectual non-existence. . . . Life becomes a perpetual revelation. This is true poetry. . . . So don't ask me to explain too clearly."

This very important example of Braque's still life lithographs gave him a great deal of trouble, particularly in the shades and proportions of the violet frame. After a number of trial proofs the impression totaled seventy-five signed and numbered prints.

The Gray Teapot, 1947.
Lithograph in six colors, 36.5 × 54 cm. Trial proof.
Published by A. Maeght, Paris.
Bibliography: Mourlot 15.
Collection Mourlot Bros., Paris.

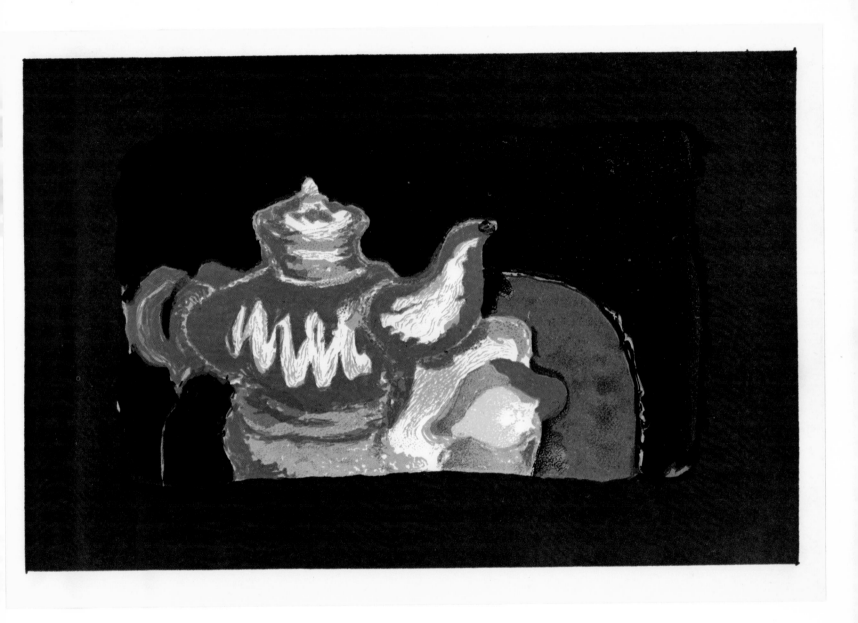

What a wonderful title for the splendid lithograph that Fernand Mourlot considers one of the finest Braque ever did! He worked on it for two years and in its first state, of which three proofs were pulled, the vase was gray, the leaves had gray ribs, and there was no frame. Braque worked over the proofs of the first state with a paintbrush before deciding on the definitive color scheme. When he had reached a decision on this point he took up the stone again and a second state was printed —first a few trial proofs and then seventy-five signed and numbered copies plus a few complimentary prints signed and marked "H.C." *(hors commerce)*.

On examining the proofs of the second state one observes first of all that the subject is greatly enhanced by the presence of a very large black frame. The gray ground has been replaced at the lower right by a patch of black spots, while the vase is much brighter thanks to its new color and still more so because the white contour line has been greatly thickened. Though the white is that of the paper, the eye does not see it as such and is attracted to it as the artist intended : it is one of the intrinsic joys of this work. In fact, the genius of the artist, who "makes the white of the paper sing," has forced it to contribute like a real color to the composition as a whole. The master engraver has made the most of it and, though we are not aware of the fact, the interplay of contrasts he has created make it seem whiter than the paper—an effect Daumier excelled at producing—or of a different tinge. Here the lithograph owes all its luminosity to this white, in which leaves and vase are immersed.

The vase of leaves with few flowers or none at all is a theme that recurs in several of Braque's prints. We find it in etchings like *Jug* of the *Cinq Sapates* (1950, Engelberts XII), *Green Bouquet* (1950,

E. 40), *Flowers* (1951, E. 41), *Ivy* (1955, E. 62), *Black Foliage* (1956, E. 66), and *Amaryllis* (1958, E. no number) in which the black leaves outlined in white on a gray ground are set in a vase placed on a table that is colored a marvelous yellow.

Bird in Foliage (Mourlot 102), which measures 104 × 80 cm, is the largest of all Braque's prints. *Leaves–Color–Light* comes next in size and is a splendid example of Braque's graphic work.

Leaves–Color–Light, 1954.
Lithograph in six colors, 97 × 60 cm. Second state. Trial proof.
Published by A. Maeght, Paris.
Bibliography: Mourlot 29.
Collection Mourlot Bros., Paris.

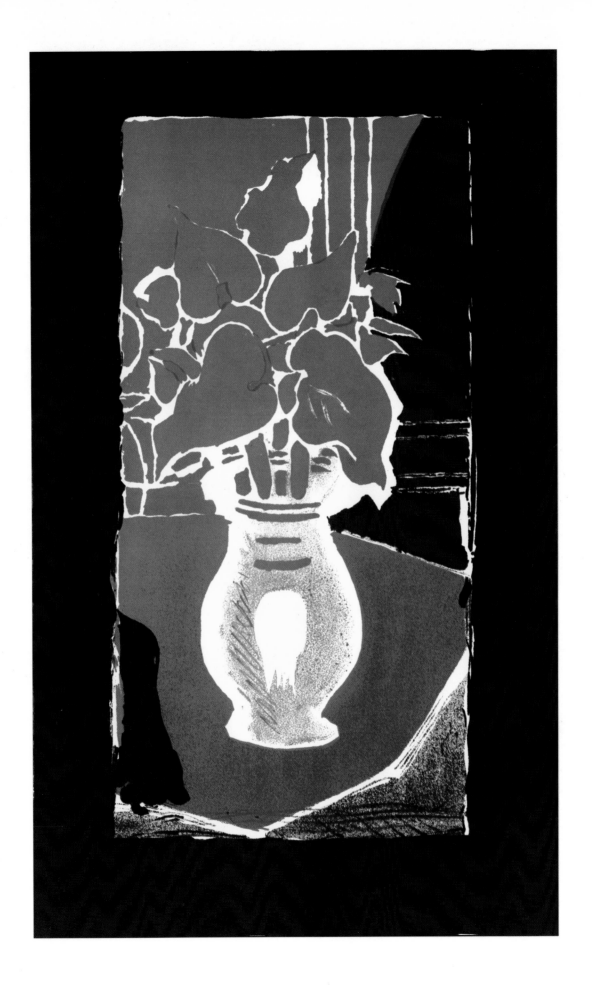

It is to the publisher Edmond Frapier that we are indebted for Utrillo's finest prints. In 1923, in fact, he asked the painter to do some lithographs for his series of albums on the *Maîtres et Petits Maîtres d'Aujourd'hui*. Utrillo was tempted by the offer and took for his subject the Parisian townscapes that had already inspired his paintings—the Cathedral of Notre-Dame, the Place du Tertre, the tavern Le Lapin Agile and other typical aspects of Montmartre. The latter include *Debray's Farm*, one of his finest prints, and *The Moulin de la Galette*, the masterpiece of them all. These lithographs were all drawn in black ink. But after the planned number of copies of the *Moulin* had been printed in black and white, a certain number of proofs were pulled in colors selected by the artist with the help of additional stones. However, contrary to the opinion of an ignorant public that demands color at all costs, the finest are those in black and white.

In 1924 Utrillo was still living in the Rue Cortot. Two years later he moved to his gilded cage on the Avenue Junot. It was still Montmartre and he was still with his mother, Suzanne Valadon, and his stepfather, the painter Utter. But he realized that his Bohemian life had come to an end. Even a single glass of wine went to his head. He spent hours at his window, which was stongly barred, looking down at the Avenue Junot and listening to the pencils he dropped as they fell one by one on the sidewalk. In his eyes one could read the dreadful despair we can see in the photographs of him.

Utrillo had long since decided, partly because he wanted to be left alone, not to paint directly from nature but only from picture postcards. In all probability he did so for this lithograph too. He had an amazing visual memory. Taking a postcard as his point of departure he plotted the classical proportions with ruler and compass. Then memory took over and all he needed to produce a masterpiece was to let his miraculous talent guide his hand.

Here he has chosen a steep lane bordered by a straggling row of sheds, behind the windmill on the Butte Montmartre, as a setting for his little figures, mostly women viewed from the rear: the women whose dray-horse buttocks led Suzanne Valadon to say, rather cuttingly "That's the only part of a woman Utrillo understands."

This lithograph went through two states. Both were printed by Duchâtel, the first in twenty copies, the second in thirty-five plus a few trial proofs. After that the stone was erased. All the prints are signed in the artist's hand "Maurice Utrillo V." The V was a compliment to the mother he adored.

The Moulin de la Galette, 1924.
Lithograph, 23.4 × 32 cm. First state. No. 1/20.
Published by E. Frapier, Paris.
Collection J. Frapier, Paris.

1/20.

Maurice, Utrillo, V.

Dunoyer de Segonzac is virtually the only great painter who was sufficiently interested in sport to give it an important place in his drawings and engravings. He had been passionately concerned with movement ever since he left his masters and struck out on his own. It was his natural reaction to the rigid, lifeless poses that models were forced to hold in art school. He was first attracted by the dance and did some fine drawings of Isadora Duncan, Ida Rubinstein and Nijinsky. Then his interest was held by boxing, particularly in the light-weight category where he found the same elegant movements as in dancers, the same concern for rhythm and balance.

All these qualities are displayed in the first state of the drypoint entitled *The Swing*. How perfectly poised on his straddled legs to deliver the blow is the boxer on the right, while his opponent, already off balance, crouches to receive it! What splendid harmony there is in this engraving, in these two men! One unwinds, all elegance and skill, swinging his trunk and arms, while the other closes his guard, mustering every effort to pull himself together and recover the balance he has already almost lost. The first is the famous American boxer Dixie Kid, middle-weight champion of the world, whose quick action earned him the nickname of "the dancing boxer."

Segonzac's first engraving dates from 1920. That explains why he never did one on the dance, which interested him chiefly before 1914. For his illustrations for Tristan Bernard's *Tableaux de la Boxe* he used a number of drawings he had done at the ringside. As in the case of his war scenes, he engraved the copperplates later. Segonzac did some sixteen hundred prints in all, and these are the only ones for which the plates were executed in the studio. All the others, including the bulk of his sporting prints, were engraved directly from nature.

In my *Homage to Dunoyer de Segonzac* I recalled that Baudelaire was struck by Delacroix's witty remark on the rendering of movement in the visual arts : "If you are not able to do a sketch of a man jumping out of a fourth-floor window by the time he reaches the ground, you will never do anything worthwhile." Segonzac possessed this rare gift to an outstanding degree. He used to quote Romain Coolus on the boxer Georges Carpentier : "It's as beautiful as Racine—the same elegance, the same style, the same measure." These words may well be applied to this engraving in which, as Claude Roger-Marx has said, it is hard to decide which is to be more admired—the boxer's fierce attack or the sure hand with which the artist has conveyed it.

The Swing, 1921.
Drypoint, 16.4 × 12.5 cm. First state. Artist's proof.
Published by N.R.F., Paris.
Bibliography: A. Lioré and P. Cailler, Vol. I, No. 48.
Private Collection.

Segonzac did one hundred and sixty-six etchings for Charles-Louis Philippe's *Bubu de Montparnasse*. Finally, however, only sixty-eight of them were used to illustrate that sensitive, sad, shrewd account of life in Paris, from street to hospital, during the early years of this century. The beauty of the illustrations makes the book one of the four most important Segonzac produced. And the finest print of all is this *Sidewalk Café*.

It is a well known fact that Segonzac does his drawings from nature directly on the copperplate just as easily as he would do a sketch on a sheet of paper. In the catalogue of the show of his three hundred and twenty five etchings at Blois Castle in 1967, I have already told an amusing story I heard from the artist himself. One day in 1923 Segonzac was walking in the valley of the Morin, carelessly dressed and carrying a load of copperplates, when he was stopped by the police, who took him for a tramp and wanted to check his parcel. Their suspicions were roused because they could not make out what he wanted the plates for. Luckily for the artist, the local innkeeper, a man called Grenier, whose wife had served Toulouse-Lautrec as a model, answered for his honesty. Luckily for us, too, because Segonzac was able to complete the splendid set of etchings known as the *Suite Morin*, engraved directly from nature in the open air, in which he has so miraculously rendered the bland charm of that corner of the Ile-de-France.

For *Bubu de Montparnasse* Segonzac followed the same procedure and sought his subjects on the scene of their activities. He wanted to capture life in the raw. So for his pimps and prostitutes he did not hesitate to seek out their haunts in the side streets round about the Boulevard Sébastopol, the Rue Saint-Denis and Les Halles (the central market). He would even go with one up to her scruffy lodgings where, on taking off her clothes, she was astonished to see him prepare his plate, and his tools, and start engraving when she obviously expected something entirely different. For his views of Paris he would sit at a table at a sidewalk café and jot down the movement of the crowd of passers, by. That is how he did this masterpiece, and I know of no other print, or even drawing for that matter, that renders with such truth the life of the Paris boulevards. Just look at the figures, barely suggested in their essentials by a few telling lines yet amazingly true to life from the working girl to the family man, from the street arab in cloth cap to the solid citizen in bowler hat. It is an evening in Paris; we are seated in the dazzling light of a crowded sidewalk café watching the whole city parade before our eyes.

Sidewalk Café, Boulevard Saint-Denis, 1929.
Etching, 33.5 × 26.6 cm. One of six trial proofs with untrimmed edges.
Bibliography: A. Lioré and P. Cailler, Vol. II, No. 191B.
Private Collection.

épreuve d'essai   pour Bubu de Montparnasse   A. Dunoyer de Segonzac

This etching is universally acclaimed as Segonzac's masterpiece. It was engraved at Saint-Tropez in 1927 and is the climax of the splendid series of *Farms with Threshing Floor*.

Segonzac discovered Saint-Tropez in 1908 when he and Luc-Albert Moreau rented lodgings there from Paul Signac. There he worked with Jean-Louis Boussingault in 1912, and it was from there that he was called to the colors on August 2, 1914. In 1926 he bought the house that belonged to the painter Charles Camoin. In 1927 he met Colette there and has returned every year since then.

The region of Saint-Tropez in Provence is one of the two poles of Segonzac's inspiration; the other is the Ile-de-France. Near "Le Maquis," his estate on the hill of Sainte-Anne, he discovered a typical Provençal farm that dated from the seventeenth century and still had the old threshing floor on which horses formerly used to trample the wheat and separate the grain from the chaff. When Segonzac showed me the floor not long ago he pointed out that its existence proved that cereals were cultivated before the vine in that part of Provence. He has a passion for the farm and its surroundings. The "beautiful motif", as he calls it, occupies an important place in his *œuvre*, whether painting, drawing or engraving, and he has worked on that motif at every hour of the day. He has done nine engravings of it. Two of the copperplates failed to please him and were erased. The other seven are very fine and include two masterpieces—*Farm with Threshing Floor, Afternoon* (Lioré and Cailler 158) and the one reproduced here.

This latter is the only one of the entire series in which human figures can be discerned. On the other hand the threshing floor itself is not visible because Segonzac sat there to engrave the plate. Before him—and the spectator—is the beautiful landscape he has made famous. The lordly cork oaks with their dark trunks stripped of the bark and their quivering, sparkling foliage frame a row of olive trees that runs down the hill towards the sea and, in the distance, a glimpse of the Maure range. In the foreground, a plough and some casks stress the Virgilian character of the magnificent Provençal scenery.

Although this engraving went through only one state, the artist worked on the plate for a longer time than was his wont. He told me that it took him four or five sittings, alternating with bitings, to finish the job. For the biting process he used baths of very weak nitric acid, so weak indeed that he sometimes let it act upon the plate the whole night long. Such multiple sittings are quite unusual for Segonzac. As a rule he dashes off his plates at one go, without a break and virtually in a single state.

The Bay of Saint-Tropez, 1927.
Etching, 27.4 × 49 cm. Press proof on antique paper.
Bibliography: A. Lioré and P. Cailler, Vol. I, No. 166.
Private Collection.

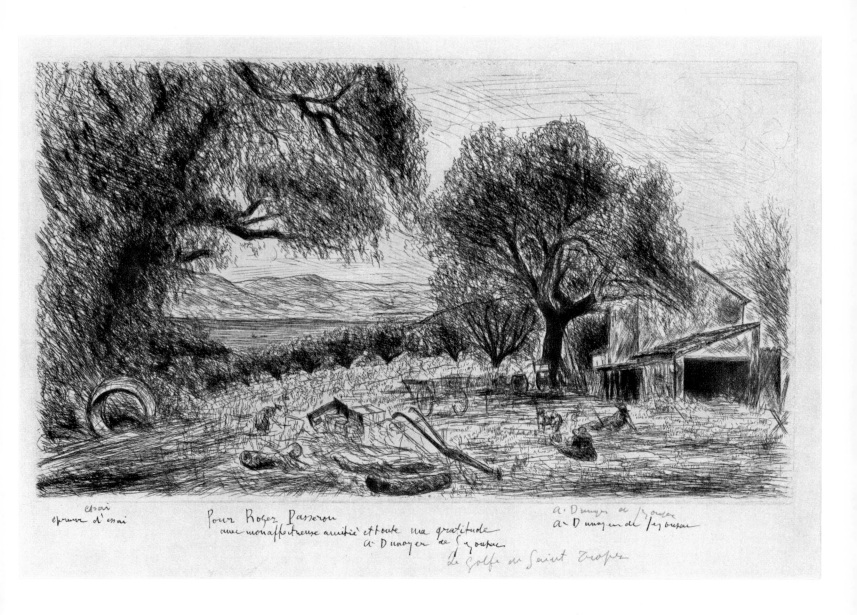

essai
épreuve d'essai

Pour Roger Passeron
avec mon affectueuse amitié et toute ma gratitude
A. Dunoyer de Segonzac

A. Dunoyer de Segonzac
A. Dunoyer de Segonzac

Le Golfe de Saint Tropez

This engraving is unfortunately extremely rare. It only exists in three proofs. A fourth was badly printed and the artist subsequently destroyed it.

In this important work—the largest etching he ever produced—Segonzac has combined three of his favorite themes : the scenery of the Provençal coast, Saint-Tropez, and the female form divine. He engraved the plate in the garden of his house, "Le Maquis", at Saint-Tropez, where he had built an artificial beach with a few cartloads of sand from Pampelone and Les Salins and where he used to go with his friend Colette to work or rest. The model is Raymonde, a lovely girl Derain was very fond of and painted several times. When Segonzac had finished the engraving he showed one of the three proofs to a friend of his, the painter Henry Coudour. The latter was obviously not at his best that day and treated the splendid print rather roughly. This made such an impression on Segonzac that he scored the plate at once, a thing he bitterly regretted later. I used this print as a poster for a show of Segonzac's graphic *œuvre* in Blois Castle because I considered it a most important work and wanted it to become more widely known.

Raymonde-Antiope is depicted here in a relaxed pose that has always been a favorite with Segonzac, whose nudes are never indecent or morbid but always natural, graceful and elegant. How natural is the attitude of this woman taking a nap in the heat of a beautiful summer day! How graceful the pose of her beautifully molded arms, to which a few deftly placed hatchings give a delightfully feminine roundness! How elegant the legs, particularly the left one with its long, slender lines!

The composition of this engraving is perfectly balanced. The female figure fills the center in a slightly diagonal position, the head resting on a sheaf of wheat. To preserve this balance, which might have been upset by the presence of the hat all by itself, the artist added a sunshade. In the two upper corners two olive trees stress this balance, framing the delightful view of the village dominated by its belfry in the middle distance with the gulf and the Maures behind it. In the foreground a Provençal bottle and two half-empty glasses, equally well balanced, and another bottle lying in a basket, await the pleasure of the artist and his model.

Thanks to the genius of Segonzac, this splendid print gives us the illusion that we are actually enjoying the peaceful atmosphere of a fine summer afternoon in the enchanting scenery of the bay of Saint-Tropez viewed from the slopes of the Sainte-Anne hill, filling our eyes with the beautiful spectacle of a comely young woman.

Antiope, 1935.
Etching, 35 × 46.5 cm. One of the three known proofs.
Bibliography: A. Lioré and P. Cailler, Vol. IV, No. 719.
Private Collection.

épreuve d'essai

Pour Roger Passeron   Antiope (une des 4 épreuves)   A. Dunoyer de Segonzac
avec ma grande reconnaissance et mon affectueuse amitié

The influence of Virgil first appears in Segonzac's landscapes about 1927. But as early as 1920 the poet Roger Allard had advised him to illustrate a Latin text for he sensed that Segonzac possessed a creative force that only the poetry of the Roman world could release.

When still a boy, Segonzac took a passionate interest in scenes of country life on his parents' estate close to Sénart Forest in the Ile-de-France. This interest has remained with him all his life long and is one of the constant factors of his inspiration. Five years ago, when I recorded on tape his invaluable comments on each of his one hundred and nineteen etchings for *The Georgics*, Segonzac insisted on the good luck that had enabled him to engrave his plates amid rural customs that had remained virtually unchanged since Virgil's times. "Today," he said, "intensive mechanization has radically modified farming and I could not possibly find in my heart the echo thanks to which I could experience and engrave what I had felt on reading Virgil and could still see before my eyes at that time both in Provence and in the Ile-de-France."

When Ambroise Vollard asked him to illustrate one of Colette's books, Segonzac, already under the impact of this Latin inspiration, suggested Virgil instead. Vollard acquiesced and fixed the format of the book. Segonzac decided on the distribution of the illustration in the Latin and French texts. He worked on the assignment steadily from 1928 to 1946. Over three hundred copperplates, all engraved directly from nature in the open air, besides watercolors, drawings and oil paintings, mark the development of his inspiration. After innumerable vicissitudes that had nothing to do with art—Vollard's death, the war, the death of Segonzac's printer Brunel, and so forth—the book was finished at long last and presented at the Galerie Charpentier, in Paris, on May 10, 1948. That occasion offered the possibility of viewing side by side the etchings that make this book one of the finest illustrated works not only of the present century but of all time.

The marvelous book comprises two volumes, each of which contains two cantos of *The Georgics*. Segonzac's love for the land, with its trees, woods and shady dells, for water and for agricultural implements makes him an enlightened disciple of Virgil. Free from all false archaism, imbued with a natural love for the simple life, the artist has rediscovered the same eternal truths that the poet sang two thousand years ago for his patron Maecenas. Given his enormous talent, Segonzac was bound to produce a masterpiece.

The splendid etching reproduced on the opposite page served as a frontispiece for Volume I. It was engraved in a vineyard close to the village of Saint-Tropez, which we can see in the distance on the right. The ox belonged to one of Segonzac's neighbors, a farmer by the name of Coulon.

The Georgics — The Grape Harvest, 1929.
Etching, 32.5 × 26.8 cm. One of the 225 proofs.
Bibliography: A. Lioré and P. Cailler, Vol. v, No. 864.
Private Collection.

André Dunoyer de Segonzac

When Marc Chagall took up engraving at the age of thirty-five in 1922, he had already produced a great many paintings. For some years he had been writing his memoirs, which were published later under the title of *Mein Leben* (My Life). They tell the story of his life and describe the people he knew, from his earliest childhood to when he left Russia. The book is written with gusto, delicacy and kindliness. Paul Cassirer, a Berlin art dealer and publisher, was greatly interested in the work and planned to publish it. So he asked Chagall to illustrate it with original engravings. Though he had never tackled a copperplate Chagall took only two or three weeks thanks to the advice he received from the engraver Hermann Struck, to do the twenty splendid etchings and drypoints plus some extra plates, which marked the starting point of a magnificent career as an engraver. This goes to show, once again, that really great painters, like Chagall, Picasso, Segonzac, Villon, Munch, to name only a few, succeed in producing masterpieces when they take up engraving for the first time.

Some thirty engravings on copper, the same number of lithographs and five woodcuts are still extant from what is called Chagall's Berlin period. On his return to Paris in the autumn of 1923 a friend of his, the writer Blaise Cendrars, introduced him to Ambroise Vollard. That great publisher realized the artist's genius at once and to the full. Proof of this is that he accepted Chagall's offer to illustrate Gogol's *Dead Souls*. What could the combination of a great Russian author and the greatest Russian artist of the present day lead to but one of the finest illustrated books published in the twentieth century ? Chagall took four years to do the plates, which put him in the forefront of contemporary engravers.

In the plates for *Mein Leben* Chagall conjured up his entire childhood—his father and mother, his grandmother and his grandfathers, the house, the street, Vitebsk, the town where he was born—with great vivacity, sensibility and absolute originality. The plates were printed in Berlin in 1922-3. The edition comprised one hundred and ten copies, the first twenty-six on Japanese vellum, the rest on hand-made laid paper. Nowadays it is very seldom one finds the whole set of twenty prints. Unfortunately the book was not published at the time because Cassirer had difficulties with the translation. In fact Chagall had written it in Russian. The engravings were published on their own in a portfolio on separate sheets collected in a hard cover.

The drypoint entitled *Grandfathers* reproduced here is the third print of the set and one of the finest. The composition recalls the Cubism Chagall had known when he first stayed in Paris before World War One. But, like Zadkine, he has interpreted it in a very personal idiom and imbued it with the human warmth that is one of the outstanding features of his entire *œuvre*.

Grandfathers, 1922.
Drypoint, 27.8 × 21.8 cm, No. 8/100 on Japanese vellum.
Published by P. Cassirer, Berlin.
Bibliography: Mein Leben, Franz Meyer; Pl. 3.
Private Collection.

81/110   Marc Chagall

Ambroise Vollard relates in his *Memoirs of an Art Dealer* that when he first became interested in publishing beautiful books illustrated by painter-engravers he felt the urge to produce a fine edition of *The Fables* of La Fontaine. When of all the artists he associated with and employed he chose Chagall for this task, it caused quite a stir because not everyone understood his idea of having a Russian illustrate the works of an essentially French author. Vollard replied that it was precisely in view of the Oriental sources of *The Fables* that he had chosen an artist whose extraction and culture brought him into close contact with that faraway, fabulous Orient. This line of argument may or may not have been correct, but in any case Vollard once again made a happy choice. The outcome was a truly magnificent book.

Vollard's first idea was to have the work illustrated with color engravings in the style of the eighteenth century. He was probably obsessed by the fame of the edition adorned with drawings by Oudry engraved in black and white by Cochin in 1755. Luckily the printer Maurice Potin was unable to "mechanize" on copper the hundred superb gouaches that Chagall produced. So the latter decided to engrave them himself, but in black and white. He did the hundred plates between 1927 and 1930. Potin printed them about that time, but the book, like so many others planned by Vollard, did not see the light until after his death : Tériade published it in 1952. The edition was limited to two hundred copies. For the first eighty-five Chagall subsequently colored a whole set of prints, perhaps with the idea of implementing Vollard's original plan.

The Raven and the Fox is the first and one of the finest of the hundred etchings. In Chagall's interpretation of the scene the poetic element, like the Raven, shelters in the branches of the tree that quivers with every one of its myriad of little leaves, which are delicately limned and poetically arranged, as are arranged in contrapuntal fashion the little dots of light produced by the sun shining through the foliage. The blacks, too, are magnificent in both the raven and the fox. And Chagall's unfailing fantasy is well in evidence : he has inverted the fox's head so that if we turn the print upside down we see Renard's arrogant, cunning mask from the same angle as does the Raven perched upon his branch.

The Raven and the Fox, 1928–29.
Etching, 29.4 × 24.7 cm. Trial proof.
Published by E. Tériade, Paris.
Bibliography: Franz Meyer, pl. 78.
Private Collection.

"It seems to me that I should have missed something, apart from color, had I not at a certain moment of my life busied myself with engravings and lithographs. . . . When I held a lithographic stone or a copperplate I believed I was touching a talisman. I felt that I could make them the repositories of all my sorrows and all my joys . . . of all the things that had crossed my life through the years : births, deaths, weddings, flowers, animals, birds, poor workers, my parents, lovers in the night, the prophets of the Bible, in the street, in the house, in the Temple, in the sky. And, with advancing years, the tragedy of life within us and round about us. . . ."

These words written by Chagall in his preface to the handsome catalogue to his lithographic *œuvre* prove how important he considers his graphic work. We have already seen that, since he did his first engraving in 1922, he has never let a year pass without producing prints. 1922-3, *Mein Leben*; 1923–7, *Dead Souls*; 1927–30, *The Fables*; 1931–9, *The Bible*—in addition to the isolated prints he did during that same period. It took the war to slow down his output in this field. But when he returned from America, where he had executed his first thirteen color lithographs, he resumed his graphic work, starting a new chapter in the Mourlots' workshop in 1950. The result to date has been over four hundred lithographs, most of them in color. Chagall reverted to lithography once he had completed his monumental task as book illustrator. And only recently Fernand Mourlot told me with what love, what study, what perseverance, he has pursued that activity alongside his work as a painter.

At Mourlot's in 1957 Chagall signed the press proof of *Circus Rider on a Red Horse* authorizing a printing of seventy-five signed and numbered copies with wide margins on Arches paper plus two thousand others for No. 9 of the review *XXᵉ Siècle*. The reader may recall that Vollard asked Chagall to illustrate a book on the circus. But the pressure of work caused by the one hundred and five engravings for *The Bible* obliged him to abandon the project. Chagall has always been greatly interested in the world of the circus and in 1923 took *The Acrobat* (Mourlot 20) as the subject of one of his earliest lithographs. Twelve lithographs in black and white and in color, some of his best, were printed by Mourlot. The one reproduced here dates from 1957. It is a magnificent climax to the prints on this theme, a crowning piece, a feast of color, of joy, of levity, of Chagallian humor. A sparkling rider stands poised on the horse, whose goatlike head expresses wit and shrewdness; she is turned towards a concealed clown, whose barely hinted features are strangely like the artist's.

Circus Rider on a Red Horse, 1957.
Lithograph in nine colors, 32 × 25 cm. Trial proof.
Published by the review *XXᵉ Siècle* (No. 9, 1957).
Bibliography: Mourlot, Vol. I, No. 191.
Collection Mourlot Bros, Paris.

On April 19, 1961, I went to see Zadkine in his studio on the Rue d'Assas in Paris to show him a set of prints for which he had found his inspiration in the war. When I opened my portfolio he was astonished to see the title—*Twenty Etchings by Osip* (sic) *Zadkine*—on the cover, and inside it his engravings in an amazingly fresh condition. Zadkine, who had never seen me before, studied me with a piercing eye under his shock of white hair. "These prints are extremely rare, my friend," he said. "As you see, I had them printed on my own account and I was very short of cash at the time. Your copy is No. 14 and must have been one of the last I managed to sell, for they were received with such indifference that I didn't continue numbering them right up to the fifty-first. All the rest were left in a corner of my studio and eventually destroyed." Acting on the spur of the moment, he wrote a dedication for me on the title page of the set where it says: "Private in the 1st foreign Regiment, seconded to the Russian ambulance with the French forces," and lower down: "On Sale at the Author's: 35 Rue Rousselet, Paris."

"I had been gassed near Epernay," he went on, "and was declared one hundred per cent incapacitated in 1917. I came home with about twenty-five drawings of war scenes, some of which are now in the War Museum at Vincennes, and got the idea of engraving a score or so to make up the set you have there." Zadkine examined his prints one by one, giving me a running commentary the while. After I had shown him the twenty-first he told me he had engraved one or two others but had not used them; consequently, as he had cut up the plates, they only existed in a very few trial proofs. My twenty-first print represented a convalescent seated with a woman in a Montparnasse café. Zadkine said it was a variant, in upright format, of the print entitled *Convalescent Playing Draughts,*

which was sited in the same café, and countersigned it under his signature of 1918.

When the catalogue of Zadkine's graphic *œuvre* was published, I realized how rare these sheets were. In fact, neither of them is mentioned there and, to make up the reproductions of the twenty etchings, the author of the work sought out one of the proofs the artist had discarded. It was entitled *The Visit* and was printed from a plate that had been cut in two. In the catalogue the cut is accounted for by "technical considerations," but that explanation does not stand up to a scrutiny of the print.

All these engravings were printed by Wittmann. They reveal a Cubist vision tempered by a very personal perspective and composition, as is the case in the prints of Chagall's Berlin period.

The One-armed N.C.O., 1918.
Etching, 14.9 × 11.7 cm, No. 14.
Bibliography: Czwiklitzer No. 1.
Private Collection.

Max Ernst has described his work as "seditious, uneven, contradictory." In a century characterized by violence, it is one of the most virulent. The artist's youth was spent in the Rhineland and was profoundly influenced by the silvan phantasmagorias of Altdorfer's engravings and the mysterious atmosphere of the strange enigmas in those Dürer produced. Ernst has never forgotten the great German romantics and metaphysicians. And all these Teutonic sources explain his career, which has been that of a rebel in every period of his artistic activity except perhaps after 1955, when his paintings reveal a certain joy.

When Ernst first reached Paris in 1919 his work created a sensation among *avant-garde* painters and writers. It was not long before he broke all his ties with Germany and became one of the leaders of the most advanced movements in Paris. Nonetheless, he never ceased being the heir to the German engravers of the fifteenth and sixteenth centuries. Their influence marked his Surrealism—which was one of the purest—and is most clearly seen in his graphic language, which aims deliberately at a well-defined objective : to reduce the spectator to a state of logical bewilderment, after a first phase of astonishment followed by one of anxiety, in order to make him receptive to the pleasure of what is out of the way and bizarre.

To achieve this result he has used not only the usual graphic techniques but also such well-known procedures as collage and frottage, for which he is famous. It was not Ernst who invented the collage : the Cubists got there first. But he used it to achieve effects that are far more disturbing, even alarming, opening up a strange, whimsical world that is at once amazing and fascinating. The juxtaposition of fragments of outmoded figures depicted in woodcuts of the turn of the century or slightly later and pasted in an odd manner in abnormal positions, served him to illustrate a fantastic universe. It served him too, in combination with unexpected page layouts, to revolutionize the illustrated book trade. Illustrations of this type, which cannot be called engravings, embellish such books as *Les Malheurs des Immortels, La Femme 100 Têtes, Une Semaine de Bonté*.

Ernst first took up engraving in 1919 with a book entitled *Fiat Modes*, which contained eight lithographs. He is also interested in etching, but only for illustrating books. His masterpiece, *Maximiliana*, was executed in 1964. He produced some fifty lithographs and about a hundred copperplate engravings between 1919 and 1965 for books alone. It was only in 1950 that he began to do separate prints and his output now totals some twenty lithographs and about the same number of etchings and aquatints, mostly in color. As a rule the line-work is nervous, original, extremely personal and, in the last few years, more serene and relaxed.

This beautiful composition of mother and child is a good example of this happy disposition. It was printed in one hundred and twenty-eight copies by Georges Visat in Paris in 1967.

Composition 1967.
Etching, 31.6 × 24.7 cm. Press proof.
Published by Galerie Gérald Cramer, Geneva.
Collection Madame Georges Visat, Paris.

BT pour Cramer   max ernst

"Gromaire : an oak that seems to have known, from the very start, that it was an oak."

Jacques Villon

Gromaire is a typical native of northern France and the impact of his ethnical origin on his art is clear to see. He was already passionately interested in drawing when he was fourteen years old. At fifteen he had already decided to become a painter once he had finished his law course at high school. On leaving school he haunted the studios of Montparnasse and was profoundly influenced by Matisse, particularly by that painter's firm line. Gromaire had no use for theory and blazed a trail of his own. If he seems close to the Expressionists, his Expressionism is solid and robust : it shows no sign of the "pathological mental disorder" that often characterizes that movement. He is fond of interpreting his subjects and giving them a rigorous linear structure that reveals a trace of Cubist influence. He delights in forms and volumes that have a monumental power and seeks his sitters among seafarers, farm workers and healthy, robust, well-built, naked young women. His painting is governed by strict graphic formulas. Gromaire has always been intensely interested in drawing both in pencil and in Indian ink. In the latter medium he favors a pure, direct handwriting, heightened by tightly packed, close hatched areas that sculpture clearly the parts in relief. So one is not surprised to find that he possesses a rare mastery of etching techniques, which serve his lyric temperament to render with the utmost vigor types of humanity that remain fixed in our memory.

It was in 1922 that Gromaire realized the potentiality of etching and first approached that medium, to which he has remained loyal ever since. His earliest plates were printed in very small editions : first twenty copies, then thirty. In 1935 he went as far as fifty; sixty around 1958 and seventy-five in 1961. From the very start he numbered the plates in addition to marking them with his monogram. He has produced some one hundred and fifty independent engravings besides those for book illustration. These latter include Baudelaire's *Petits Poèmes en Prose* (1926), Emmanuel's *Memento des Vivants* (1944) and Aloysius Bertrand's *Gaspard de la Nuit*. In 1958 Tériade commissioned the illustrations for an edition of *Macbeth*.

This *Man with Spade* was engraved in 1927 and printed in thirty copies. It is one of the finest products of contemporary engraving and a perfect example of Gromaire's art for it displays all his force and skill. The peasant, firmly planted on legs that seem rooted in the soil he has been digging, merely pauses a moment to light his pipe. The horizon is low and the man towers like a statue in the vast wintry sky above the flat countryside. He is a typical peasant whose land is his life, and seems to protect his village which is symbolized by a few houses huddling in the shadow of the belfry. This print is truly a gem.

Man with Spade, 1927.
Etching, 23.8 × 18 cm, No. 14/30.
Bibliography: P. Cailler, pl. 74 (not yet published).
Collection Marcel Lecomte, Paris.

Gromaire

14/30

In 1959 Jacques Villon wrote in his *Grand Testament*: "...I think that when thousands and thousands of years have passed engraving will still bear witness to the presence of man. Painting will be reduced to a drawing of expression and opinion, a simplified drawing that imitates engraving...." A few years earlier Joan Miró, whose point of departure was a different horizon, had developed a different line of thought in these words: "...in the last few years we have seen a sort of renascence of craftsmanly means of expression: pottery, lithography, wood engraving, etching.... All these art forms, which are less costly than painting and often make an equally authentic plastic statement, will increasingly occupy the place of painting...."

It would be wrong to crassly oppose painting and engraving for on the contrary the two arts mutually fertilize each other. But it is interesting to observe cursorily how these two great artists agree in the important place they assign to engraving. This explains how it is that they are both passionately interested in that branch of art and have devoted a great deal of time to it. Miró in particular gives us ample proof of this. In 1930 he did four lithographs to illustrate *L'Arbre des Voyageurs*. But it was not until 1944, when he produced the splendid set of fifty plates entitled *Barcelona*, that he really took up engraving in a big way. In the fifteen years that followed he did over four hundred etchings, lithographs and woodcuts.

One cannot understand Miró's *œuvre* properly if one ignores the fact that he is a Catalan. Catalonia, which has always dominated the other Spanish provinces where art is concerned, was the cradle of the Romanesque style and from the start Miró fed on the daring colors of the paintings in its churches and the forceful stylization of its sculptures. It is to the gaiety of Catalan folk art and to his own popular vocation that he owes his fresh, childish vision and he has often found inspiration in the ideograms of children's paintings. Later, in Paris, Surrealism made no mark upon him for he lived it naturally, but it brought his art to maturity. As André Breton said, "Miró is probably the most Surrealist of us all."

It is no easy matter to explain the spell that Miró's works have always cast on the beholder. In them there is no form but a mass of embryos, amoebae, rudimentary foetal figures that put us forcibly in mind of the happy, spontaneous scrawls children make in the full freedom of their pure, disinterested inspiration. Moons—red, yellow, green or blue—shapeless, black, protozoan lumps, corded placentas, an entire biology in studied disorder which on closer examination reveals a rigorous, harmonious construction. All this dream world is present in the lithograph reproduced here. It is quite typical of Miró and was printed by Mourlot in 1955 in seventy-five signed copies on Arches paper.

The Melancholy Traveler, 1955.
Lithograph in six colors, 76 × 56 cm.
Published by A. Maeght, Paris.
Private Collection.

Goerg is a painter who devotes much of his time to engraving. After he had etched a great many plates from which a small number of prints were pulled, he took up lithography. He excels in fantastic scenes.

I have selected a color lithograph entitled *The Three Graces* to represent Goerg in this book because I find that the expressions of the three girls' faces are very typical of the artist. They reveal the mixture of candor, naïvety, artfulness and perverseness we find in Nabokov's *Lolita*.

It was in the Galerie Sagot-Le Garrec that I met Goerg for the first time. We chatted about Daumier and I voiced my enthusiasm for that master's lithographs, with their deep, velvety blacks and rich, creamy whites. "Quality of that sort cannot be obtained nowadays," he said, and went on to tell me of his particular veneration for Daumier, Goya and Rouault. These three names explain Goerg's realistic bent. But he has added a touch of sentimentality that is all his own. He has evolved towards naturalism and one of the major features of this phase is the representation of very young, barely nubile girls. The dramatic component of the theme is emphasized, particularly in his engravings, by his skilful rendering of contrasts.

Goerg told me that the lithograph reproduced here was commissioned by a Swiss publisher who scared him by demanding a very large number of prints. In fact the edition totaled two hundred copies plus some twenty artist's proofs. Being accustomed to very limited editions, Goerg was rather uneasy. Actually, that was quite unwarranted because, as he told me last year, the entire edition was sold out a long time ago. He added that this was not his first color lithograph, though it dated from the time he took up that medium. From his friend, Jacques Villon, whose color lithographs he greatly admired, he received invaluable advice.

Goerg also admitted his debt to the lithographic printer Edmond Desjobert.

This lithograph was produced using five different stones—one for the black and four for the colors (green, red, ocher and yellow). Goerg said that four colors plus black were quite enough to render his vision and insisted that the delicate problem of registering the stones for the successive impressions was easier to solve when there were not more than five stones.

The Three Graces, 1950.
Lithograph in five colors, 43.5 × 30.5 cm, No. 124/200.
Published by La Guilde de la Gravure, Geneva.
Private Collection.

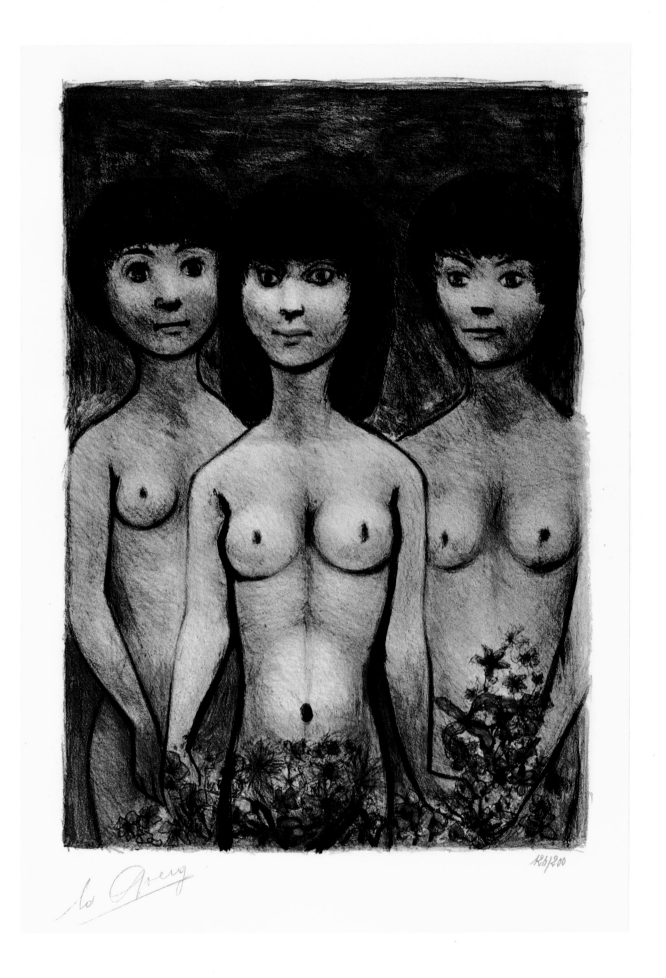

"And if ever the sun, which has never set, should set, *aurora borealis* and mirage, it will live on in the universe of André Masson."   *Robert Desnos*

Masson has devoted a large part of his artistic activity to engraving and has obtained amazingly rich effects by techniques he invented himself. Not long ago he told me of the joy he felt every time he witnessed the metamorphosis of the foaming acid that changes color during its violent reaction with the metal. He insisted repeatedly on the fascination that reaction had for him. And Jacques Frélaut has related how Masson spent hours on end engraving in his (Frélaut's) workshop, without counting the time, until deep into the night.

Masson's first engravings were three etchings that date from 1924 when Kahnweiler asked him to illustrate a book of poems by Georges Limbour entitled *Soleil bas*. He told me later that since then he had done over five hundred prints, part separate plates, part book illustrations, of which two-thirds are in color and more than half are lithographs.

For many years Masson was intensely interested in mythology. It was the myth of Sisyphus that inspired this splendid plate, which was printed in thirty copies. It was engraved in 1946 and went through three states. The first was done in dry-point throughout and the copperplate was very large (43 × 63.4 cm) because on the left, from top to bottom and to a width of 9 centimetres, the artist engraved a number of observations : a rock, a first self-portrait facing left, a second self-portrait facing right, another, more highly worked-up stone resembling a crouching ram. Masson told me that he removed these sketches in the second state by cutting the copperplate, which he then worked over in aquatint. Lastly, for the third state, which is reproduced here, he added some more touches in aquatint.

On the left we can see the rock god whose thundering voice pronounces the sentence; on the right, the son of Aeolus labors under the absurd yoke, hoisting his stone, which disintegrates under the implacable eye of the god and whose fragments fall at his feet just as he thinks he is reaching his goal. The black ground of the aquatint represents the inky darkness of Hell, in which Sisyphus is fated to toil for all eternity.

André Masson is a sensitive artist and a pleasant, cultivated person, who aims at expressing a vigorous revolt and an unremitting quest for the impossible, rather than at producing a pure work of plastic art. This engraving is very typical of the man who wrote : "I must always preserve in my painting the imprint of a certain wild nature. Something like a torrent."

Sisyphus, 1946.
Drypoint and aquatint, 42.3 × 54.1 cm, No. 4/20.
Published by Galerie Louise Leiris, Paris.
Galerie Paul Prouté, Paris.

In his *Diary of a Genius*, a memoir very typical of the Spanish artist, Salvador Dali relates that when he was asked to do a set of lithographs to illustrate *The Adventures of Don Quixote* he was greatly prejudiced against that medium. The reasons for this were aesthetic, moral and philosophical, for he considered that lithography lacked rigor, monarchy and an inquisition. In his eyes that technique was liberal, bureaucratic and flaccid. As a matter of fact, he goes on to say that he changed his mind when his editor's insistence irritated his anti-lithographic convictions to the point of aggressive hyper-aesthesia. It was at this point that an angelic idea dazzled the jaws of his brain. Instantaneously, like an angel, he controlled the situation of his Quixote. From Puerto Lligat he wired Paris to make ready an harquebus for his arrival so that he could fire it at a lithographic stone. His friend, the painter Georges Mathieu, made him a present of a fifteenth-century weapon. From a barge on the Seine Dali created history by firing a ball filled with lithographic ink at a stone, causing a divine splash, a sort of angel's wing, whose aerial details and dynamic rigor surpass all the techniques hitherto employed. It would be a mistake to believe that in the matter of technical innovation Dali's genius limited its action to lithography. Etching also claimed his attention : he utilized the automatic gesture drawing of a live sea-urchin's quill linked with a point to etch a plate under the control of his own sensitive whiskers.

One cannot, however, ignore Dali's graphic *œuvre* when his genius is satisfied with more orthodox techniques. As all the world knows, the illustrator of *Les Chants de Maldoror* (published by Albert Skira in 1934 with forty-two etchings by Dali) is not only one of the greatest painters of the twentieth century : he is also a very great draughtsman. Drawings like the one he did of his father and sister in 1925 and still more his portrait drawing of René Crevel entitled *The Man with the Cigarette* (1934)—to mention only two—are genuine masterpieces. This explains how it is that Dali has produced so many etchings, aquatints and lithographs. Particularly noteworthy among his prints are the views of Paris. In 1963 he did *Place de la Concorde* with a splendid lion, *Les Invalides* and the *Porte Saint-Denis*. But the finest of them all is this *Place des Vosges* executed in 1958.

This aquatint was preceded by a large drawing heightened with wash. It went through three states before the copperplate was cut to size and beveled. The printing totaled one hundred and twenty-five copies on special paper with Dali's watermark. In 1965 the plate had not yet been scored.

Place des Vosges, 1958.
Etching and aquatint, 44.7 × 59.3 cm.
Private Collection.

Robert Blanchet, one of the leading woodcut printers of our day and a pupil of Jacques Beltrand, asked Lorjou to illustrate a book for him. Lorjou had already produced some fifty lithographs and over thirty etchings. He got the idea of taking up wood engraving and, being an animal lover, thought of doing Guillaume Apollinaire's *Bestiaire*. The book had already offered Dufy an opportunity to do a set of splendid woodcuts in black and white. Lorjou was intensely interested in color and instinctively chose the color woodcut as his medium. It took him two years to produce an extraordinary work. As he told me himself during a conversation we had in his studio, "for me the success of that enterprise depended on taking it in hand with absolute intellectual and technical freedom, as the spirit moved me. Without any preliminary plan, without keeping too slavishly to the text. Anyway, I am convinced that it is more interesting to illustrate poems than prose, for a poem is more abstract and leaves the illustrator a freer hand. Each word of a poem creates an image and provides the artist with a richer lode. One must read the poem, let an idea be born, and transpose it spontaneously to the woodblock in order to preserve all its freshness. Of course that is no easy matter : the wood resists and defends itself against the drive of hand and hammer; it may even split and then the artist must discover a remedy, take advantage of the fault and turn what seemed a vexatious contingency into a felicitous invention. Since the woodcut is a simple medium one is forced to think simply. Lastly, and above all, one must not get bogged down in the traditions and tricks of the trade. One must not be afraid to take a chance, for if one is in the right frame of mind the chance can be lucky. There are involuntary points of contact with the poem that are the harmonics of the major theme : the chance grain of the wood, which one must not stop up when inking the block but rather allow to breathe for it offers an extraordinary motif. All this is done as the work proceeds. One cannot decide in advance. As Blanchet told me one day, 'You don't know what you are going to do!' That's lucky, for otherwise I would be bored and consequently I would bore Apollinaire."

The marvelous book is illustrated with thirty-three color woodcuts for which Lorjou had to sculpt over one hundred and fifty blocks. It took three blocks to produce the *Goat*. A blue block with the animal scooped out with a gouge; a pink block with the outline in relief, and a third block printed in green with the goat "reserved." The superimpression of these blocks resulted in a fourth color—a dull pink.

In 1965 two hundred and thirty copies of the book were printed by Blanchet besides fifty sets of engravings on Richard de Bas paper with wide margins signed and numbered by the artist.

Apollinaire's Goat, 1964.
Woodcut in three colors, 34.3 × 24.4 cm, No. 23/50.
Published by Editions d'Auteuil, 1965.
Private Collection.

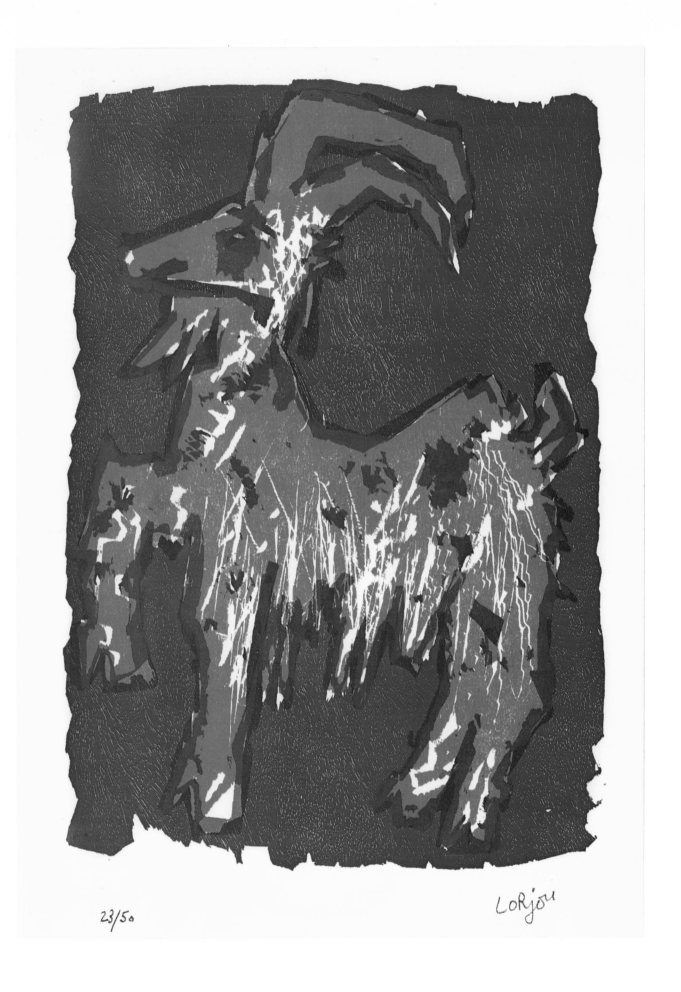

23/50

LoRjou

Manessier underwent various influences and teachings that left their mark on the development of his art towards its maturity. He first attended the Ecole des Beaux-Arts at Amiens, then he got a solid grounding in architecture at the Académie Ranson, after which he studied under Roger Bissière. Most important of all was a period he spent at the Trappe in 1943. These different stages enable us to understand the orientation of his artistic production.

His stay in the Trappist monastery when he was still a young man made a deep impression on him and from then on he gave his religious art the abstract expression that is spiritually the highest. "It seems to me," he says, "that at present non-figurative art offers the best possible chance for a painter to recover his reality. If man is a hierarchy of values, his outer appearance is nothing but a transparent phantom if it is devoid of spiritual content." Manessier has exerted a considerable influence on the renovation of sacred art and some religious Orders see in him one of the leaders responsible for a movement based on spiritualized abstraction. As he himself said to Dom Angelico Surchamp, "personally, I do a sort of painting that matches my thirst for harmony and unity, my urge to climb back step by step towards a rebuilt me, towards the lost world of grace. But this painting is quite alien to the public for the public lives in a materialistic world and no longer discovers this need in itself. . . ."

Manessier's architectural studies enabled him to grasp the rigorous, logical structure of Cubism and discover it from a new angle. Fauvism taught him that color comes first—a rich, brilliant color to which after 1943 he added a spiritual intensity. Since then in his eyes color is light and light is first and foremost a vector of spirituality. "Light is the great bond," he often says.

Like Rouault, another great religious artist, Manessier has always been fascinated by stained glass windows. He has done some very fine specimens himself, for he was led naturally and intimately to take up this splendid art by his passion for color and light, by his knowledge of architecture, and by his religious fervor. After enriching stained glass through his skill and sensibility as a painter, he drew from it an enrichment for his painting and engraving. Manessier could not possibly have ignored lithography and the light which that medium receives from the paper. We are indebted to him for splendid sets of lithographs on the themes of Easter and the *Spiritual Canticles* of St. John of the Cross. This *Live Flame* is one of Manessier's finest productions in that technique. It was inspired by a poem by St. John of the Cross and was printed in one hundred and seventy-five copies by Mourlot in 1957.

Live Flame, 1957.
Lithograph in five colors, 51.4 × 35.5 cm. Artist's proof.
Published by L'Œuvre Gravé, Locarno.
Bibliography: Catalogue Nesto Jacometti No. 121.
Galerie Sources, Paris.

épreuve d'artiste   Manessier

Antoni Clavé is the youngest of the four Spanish engravers represented in this book. He first approached engraving through lithography on his arrival in Paris in 1939. In Barcelona, at the start of his career, he had sold some drawings to illustrate magazines and periodicals besides doing publicity drawings and experimenting with collage. Since then Clavé has chiefly produced lithographs in color and in black and white. He has illustrated a number of books, such as Prosper Mérimée's *Lettres d'Espagne* in 1943, *Chansons du Passé du XVᵉ au XVIIIᵉ Siècle* in 1944, *Carmen* and *Le Carrosse du Saint Sacrement* by Mérimée, *La Dame de Pique* by Pushkin and *Candide* by Voltaire in 1946.

In 1950 he started work on the lithographs for the finest book he has illustrated so far, *Gargantua* by Rabelais, which is also one of the finest published in the twentieth century. It comprises some sixty lithographs in several colors and a great many chapter headings designed by Clavé and engraved in wood by Blaise Monod. All the ornaments, typographical signs and pen strokes were designed by Clavé. The lithographs are admirable for drawing, composition and coloring, as you can see from this one which illustrates the chapter where Rabelais enumerates the exercises Gargantua must do to become a "perfect knight": "... (they) went out of their house, and with them a young gentleman of Touraine, named the esquire Gymnast, who taught him the art of riding. Changing then his clothes he rode a Naples courser ... then a light fleet horse, made him go the high saults, bounding into the air, free a ditch with a skip, leap over a style.... Then would he hunt the hart, the roebuck, the bear, the fallow deer, the wild boar, the hare, the partridge, the pheasant and the bustard.... He did cast the dart, throw the bar, put the stone, practise the javelin, the boar spear and the halbert. He drew the strongest bows, bended against his breast the greatest cross-bows of steel, took his aim by the eye with the hand-gun, and shot well.... from below upwards, from above downwards, then before him sideways, and behind him like the Parthians."

Clavé used eight colors for this lithograph which demanded the successive impression of eight stones. It was printed by the lithographic printers Edmond and Jacques Desjoberts of Paris. In the throes of creative activity for a subject in which he took a passionate interest, Clavé used thin brushes for the black linework, thick brushes for the flat tints, and finished the plate with his fingers as we can see from the traces of finger prints they left. He added some touches of wide-mesh lace that are visible on the plumes of the knight's helmet and on the horse's mane.

The splendid book, which is characterized by a truly Rabelaisian truculence, was printed in two hundred and twenty copies. It later provided the inspiration for some very large color lithographs —the famous *Kings* series. The great painter-engraver has also done etchings and is busy at present on some sumptuous color aquatints.

The Knight Hunting, 1950.
Lithograph in eight colors, 35 × 24 cm.
Published by Les Bibliophiles de Provence.
Private Collection.

"In my study at Malagar a man's face drawn by Michel Ciry looks at me and I do not know whether the eyes he fixes on me condemn or pardon me. For this man is Christ—I know it—though not one of his features resembles the image of the Son of God that tradition has imposed on sculptors and painters from one century to the next. . . ."
François Mauriac, Nouveaux Mémoires intérieurs
(Flammarion)

This is one of François Mauriac's comments on an engraving that made a very deep impression on him, as it did on me when I discovered it in 1956 in a print dealer's shop on the Rue de Seine. At that time I had never even heard of Michel Ciry. Four years later, when I began to compile the catalogue of his graphic *œuvre*, I studied this etching in great detail and found out that it had gone through twelve states—a thing Ciry himself had never realized.

It is intensely interesting to trace the artist's progress from state to state in an attempt to fix his thought, his inner vision of Christ. The Christ of the concentration camp era, who has suffered His Passion and returns to fix us with these supernaturally intense eyes in which we can read love, self-sacrifice, a sorrowful reproach and the radiant kindness that leads us to expect mercy. From one state to the next a few hatchings or cross-hatchings, a few touches, alter the initial expression, change the direction of the gaze, accentuate its intensity, express spirituality, hint at the insults received and the pangs endured.

This etching, which was engraved in 1949, is an important landmark in Michel Ciry's graphic *œuvre*. He had already engraved many sacred themes but had never achieved an expression of such intensity. Never before had he rendered such spirituality, such lofty, grave emotion. Since then Ciry's inter-est has centered on the human face and in paintings, drawings and engravings he has joined the number of great artists who have succeeded in making it express the sublime sentiments of spiritual life.

This etching was printed in fifty numbered copies plus a few artist's proofs by Georges Visat in Paris. In view of the importance of the work I advised Ciry to have a second printing of fifteen artist's proofs made. It was done in Jacques Frélaut's workshop in Paris. I then purchased the copperplates and had holes bored in the four corners to make sure that no further impressions could be taken against the artist's will.

Jesus, 1949.
Etching, 23.9 × 17.9 cm. Twelfth state. No. 6/50.
Bibliography: R. Passeron, Vol. IV, No. 727.
Private Collection.

6/50

MICHEL CIRY 1949

Julien Green, the novelist, after visiting a show of Ciry's works, wrote to the artist to tell of his enthusiasm. In the last paragraph of his letter he insisted on the "unforgettable gaze" he gave his sitters, "whose eyes say far more than many books." And he closed with these words : "You must be happy to be so wonderfully gifted, as I am happy to insist once again on my admiration and my friendship."

This friendship was the outcome of mutual admiration. Long before they had met, the artist counted the writer among his favorite authors together with Montherland and Mauriac. In 1955 he did forty-one etchings to illustrate Green's *Voyageur sur la Terre* and their sympathy soon developed into friendship. Those who know how reserved they both are realize from this how deep is their mutual esteem.

In 1961 Ciry engraved the face of a Franciscan monk on a copper plate. He had long been inspired by the strong personality of St. Francis and his graphic *œuvre* comprises many proofs of this devotion, from the *Fioretti* he engraved when he was nineteen to the *St. Francis* of 1967. Two proofs were pulled from this plate. They form the first state of the engraving. But when Ciry read Green's *Chaque Homme dans sa Nuit* he felt a new inspiration and, taking up his plate again, turned the monk into a layman—a plain man like any one of us. After nine states he succeeded in rendering his vision and the result was this splendid print, to which he gave the title of the novel that had inspired it. It pays homage to Julien Green.

In this etching Ciry has personified Wilfred, the hero of the novel, by the depth of the gaze and the lighting behind the Surrealist veil. Above and beyond the character himself, he has evoked the major themes of Green's work. In his night, in his solitude, this man resists the incessant temptations that surround him and accompany him along his way. But there is a certainty that sustains him, for "every man in his night advances towards his light," and for him this light is a light that is never extinguished. How wonderful is an art that enables an engraver to express, with a point on a copper-plate, such profound sentiments, such intense life, such noble certainties. The gentleness of the gaze, the will it expresses to resist temptation, all this is amazing and makes the work one of Michel Ciry's masterpieces.

It was printed in fifty numbered copies and a few artist's proofs by Jacques Frélaut.

Every Man in his Night, 1961.
Etching, 25.9 × 16.9 cm. Ninth state. No. 8/50.
Bibliography: R. Passeron, Vol. V, No. 916.
Private Collection.

8/50

MICHEL CIRY 1961

Mario Avati has always been fond of animals and they occupy an important place in his drawings and engravings.

In a letter written in August 1957, two months after our first meeting, Avati told me that he spent whole days at the Vincennes Zoo where, "drawing madly," he piled up hundreds of sketches of animals done from life. When I came back from my vacation he showed me those sketches, some of which are highly finished works. They made up a splendid bestiary and I was enthusiastic about them. He also showed me some large drawings done in his studio after the sketches. One represented eight zebras. An American was struck by the beauty of the theme and asked him to do an engraving of it. Avati was tempted but hesitated for a long time before coming to a decision. In the end the engraving, though based on the original drawing, was entirely different from it : instead of eight zebras standing still, the aquatint shows us six zebras on the run.

The chief reason for Avati's hesitation in the first place was the large format, which was quite unusual for him in 1957. But in engraving as everywhere else the need to surmount an obstacle acts as a challenge, and the outcome was one of Avati's masterpieces. It is worth noting that the technical difficult intrinsic in engraving, which painter-engravers are forced to overcome, instead of hampering their inspiration and hindering their creative drive, sublimates them and makes them work miracles—subject, of course, to the condition that they are true masters.

On this plate Avati first drew the outline of his zebras with a point. Then, reserving the whites with a varnish, he used a very strong acid to bite the entire surface of the copper, including the zebras' black stripes, over which he had strewn grains of resin to produce a graded effect—a sort of milky way—on three corners of the plate. A second, more diluted, acid bath acted on the whites, chiefly along the outlines of the animals' bodies, in order to produce relief. Lastly, the aquatint biting process was repeated fifteen times on the background in order to obtain the magic, warm black that is a no less important factor in the beauty of this engraving than the splendid composition of the herd of zebras in motion.

The print went through three states : a few trial proofs on blue, yellow, red and Arches paper and on Japanese vellum, followed by fifty numbered copies all of which were sold in the United States. Avati kept only ten artist's proofs and the trial prints for his own use. Both the proofs and the final edition were printed by Rigal in 1957. Mr Chaïkin presented the plate to the French National Library and it is now kept in the office of the Chief Curator of the Print Room.

Six Running Zebras . . . , 1957.
Aquatint, 44.5 × 60.5 cm. Fourth state. Unique proof on Japanese vellum No. 1/1.
Published by the artist. Edition bought by Mr Nathan Chaïkin, USA.
Bibliography: R. Passeron, Vol. I, No. 214 (not yet published).
Private Collection.

SIX ZEBRES COURANT...   AVATI

Avati produced some thirty prints—etchings, dry-points, aquatints and lithographs—before venturing on the mezzotint in 1950. His first cautious experiment in this technique was a delightful little engraving entitled *The Little Fool* (R. Passeron 33). It dates from the period when Avati was obsessed by people's faces and on studying it we can understand that he realized what vast possibilities the mezzotint offered him. He continued his researches for six years, producing twenty-two prints in that medium and one hundred and sixty-six in the others which, except perhaps for lithography, he by no means neglected.

In March 1956 Avati did *Still Life with Olives* (R. P. 200), the first of his masterly mezzotints in large format. Marcel Lecomte, the well known dealer and connoisseur, called my attention to this work and through him I met the artist. Since then Avati has done over a hundred mezzotints and one is justified in saying that today he leads the world where that technique is concerned. He has attained an amazing mastery in this field and this skill has enabled him to dominate the incredible virtuosity of his handling to the point where all one sees is the expression of his feelings and all one realizes is the immense quality of his art. In fact, though the mezzotint is not a popular medium, many other artists have employed it to produce some extremely fine prints. But, with few exceptions, those works are feats of skill that demonstrate their dexterity and nothing more.

When the mezzotint was invented in the seventeenth century it was used chiefly for portraits by German engravers first and English afterwards. Today it is employed rather for still lifes. But the objects presented in these compositions, though handsomely engraved in the best cases, are often jumbled together without rhyme or reason, without unity, without a soul. Avati endows his with an extra dimension—the mystery of their inner life, which he brings out by means of an unusual lighting, at once subtle and supernatural, giving them a spiritual factor which recalls Chardin. What makes us realize and appreciate the beauty of Avati's mezzotints is the quality of the silence that pervades them and what Roger Brielle, a painter and a great friend of Paul Eluard, Pierre Reverdy and André Breton, used to call their surreality.

Still Life with Artichokes was engraved together with two other plates at the request of the great American collector Fred Grunwald who, when he died in 1964, owned three hundred and fifty-three prints by Avati. He left them to the Grunwald Graphic Arts Foundation at the University of California (Los Angeles).

The work went through five states. It was printed in seventy-five numbered copies and twelve artist's proofs by Rigal, the best printer of Avati's mezzotints. Grunwald presented his friends with the seventy-five numbered copies for Christmas 1956.

Still Life with Artichokes, 1959.
Mezzotint, 21.5 × 24.6 cm. Unique proof of the fourth state before steel-plating.
Published by the artist. Edition purchased by Mr F. Grunwald, USA.
Bibliography: R. Passeron, Vol. II, No. 258 (not yet published).
Private Collection.

4: ETAT ⅛

AVATI 79

Lars Bo is a Danish painter-engraver who has made his home in Montmartre since 1947. In July 1963 he spent some time in a little village in the Aisne Department that was exceptionally ugly and devoid of charm. Its sole attraction was the nightingales, which were still singing despite the lateness of the season. Every night a song of wondrous purity filled the darkness that sheathed the house where Bo was staying. When the moon rose, silvering the leaves of the trees, the song swelled till it seemed to fill the world.

Back in Paris, Lars Bo was obsessed by the memory of that song: through September and October he worked on this magnificent print. He told me that it demanded two plates. The master plate bears the drawing. The other, which was put through the press first, was inked in two or three colors—the brownish red of the background, the rather lighter red of the bird and the pale green of the trees. The master plate was printed in a very dark green that keeps its color in the weak aquatint and goes black in the thick lines—for instance, the shadows of the trees—which are engraved with a burin. This analysis of the artist's procedure interested me greatly and I asked him through how many states the print had gone. "I don't know exactly," he replied, "for I did not keep count, but there must have been nearly thirty trial and state proofs." Then Bo asked me a question in his turn: "Every time one tries out a color does that constitute a state in the proper sense of the term? One lightens the green a little and pulls a proof: is that a state? Then I work over the plate with a drypoint, deepening a few of the lines. Another proof is pulled: that is a state. I take up the color plate again to shade a red; another proof is pulled. And this continues until I am quite satisfied or else destroy the whole thing. In the throes of the creative process I am not completely aware of the phases of the procedure. In the case of a color engraving these phases are inevitably very numerous. One gets sudden ideas that can sometimes radically alter the original idea. That is the source of the joy I feel. An inexhaustible source of joy: creation, surprise, harmony."

This aquatint was printed by Rigal in eighty numbered copies plus ten others on Japanese vellum, in addition to a few artist's proofs. It was a great success in Paris, Tokyo, New York, Geneva, Stockholm and Oslo. Jacques Frapier chose it as the poster for an exhibition in the Galerie des Peintres-Graveurs. It was also used for the same purpose for shows in the Far Gallery, New York, and the Micklesens Gallery, Washington.

The Nightingale's Song, 1963.
Color aquatint, 35.5 × 47.4 cm, No. 52/80.
Published by J. Frapier, Paris.
Private Collection.

un chant du Rossignol —

Several years ago Mario Avati told me of the great hopes he placed in the work of a young artist named Ramondot, who had not only exceptional gifts as an engraver but also—which is rarer still—a novel inspiration.

In May 1962 Jean-Claude Romand organized a show of Ramondot's engravings that enabled those who saw it to form an opinion of his art. An outstanding exhibit was the fine print reproduced here.

The artist told me later that it was the result of a chance experience. During a journey to Italy he was struck, one night at San Gimignano, by a butcher's shop that still had the light on though it was after closing time. The crude lighting, striped by the horizontal slats of the shutters, gave breadth to a scene that otherwise would have been commonplace—though actually Rembrandt and Soutine have given us ample proof that that adjective is not well suited where flayed beef carcasses are concerned. The unusual spectacle touched off Ramondot's artistic sensibility. He made a rapid sketch and took a snapshot to supply reference points for his memory. The majestic proportions of the carcass spread out like a gigantic butterfly, the contrast between this violently illuminated mass of meat and the geometric design of the tiled floor, the counter and the walls clad with black and white marble slabs, made a deep impression on him, as did the harmonious combination of the well-cleansed anatomy with the decorative elements of the shop. The latter seemed just the right size for the huge frames of Tuscan oxen. "A box for an ox," is how the artist described it. And above all the fascination of the bright red flesh that had already inspired so many great artists to produce masterworks.

This took place in August 1955. During the following winter, which Ramondot spent at the Villa Medici in Rome, he recomposed the subject in drawings. A first engraving entitled *The Big Butcher's Shop* done in March 1956 respected the composition of the scene but failed to capture the emotion he had felt. In the same month he did a second etching and in November 1961 the definitive drypoint. The square format and the velvety effect of the medium employed, which provides an aura of mystery due to the tools (steel, ruby or diamond) used directly on the copperplate, finally gave the artist what he was looking for.

The engraving went through three states—two proofs were pulled of each—before steel-plating. After that process six artist's proofs and fifty numbered copies were printed (the printing was still incomplete in 1968). In order to obtain an effect of transparency, the artist asked the master printer Camille Quesneville to add a drop of ultramarine to the black ink.

Beef, 1961.
Drypoint, 38.9 × 38.8 cm. Third state. One of the two proofs before steel-plating.
Private Collection.

EPREUVE D'ESSAI AVANT ACIERAGE   BOEUF   Jacques
                                                                           RAMONDOT

Buffet has already produced over three hundred drypoint engravings and almost one hundred lithographs. This ensemble is as unique in the field of twentieth-century print making as his paintings are in that of contemporary painting.

When Buffet plans to do an engraving he is not afraid to tackle a very large plate. Indeed, it is worth noting that all his finest prints are comprised among those of largest size. *The Steeple at Sauzon* reproduced here; *School* (Reinz 130) of 1953; *La Rochelle Harbor* (R. 156) and *Breton Seaport* (R. 157) of 1954; *Rabbit* (R. 179) of 1955; *Toad* (R. 183) of 1957; *Semaphore* (R. 228) of 1959; *Rhoténeuf Lighthouse* (R. 249) of 1961; *Gazelle* (R. 272) of 1962; *Canal at Soissons* (R. 282) of 1964; and *Hôtel de la Poste* (R. 287) of 1965 were printed from plates that ranged from 50 × 65 cm to 54 × 72 cm. These engravings are Buffet's masterworks in this field and were all executed exclusively with the drypoint technique. In fact—and it is worth while insisting on this—where the engraved area of the copperplate is concerned they are the largest drypoints ever produced. Copper and point offer the artist's impetuous temperament a means of expression that employs his creative force at full stretch and renders with extreme vigor the most intimate aspects of his vision. Jacques Frélaut, who prints Buffet's engravings, told me that his plates are so deeply worked that they cannot be printed without a pause: the burrs are so big that they soon lacerate skin of the hand used to rub the plate after inking.

Buffet has always been fascinated by the sea and his engravings include many seascapes. One of his finest illustrated books is Baudelaire's *La Mer*, for which he transcribed the text on the copperplates in his own hand; it is illustrated with seascapes in the Saint-Cast district. *The Steeple of Sauzon* was also engraved after a Breton port. It is one of the two or three finest engravings Buffet has done so far.

Here the inhuman immobility of Buffet's landscapes is attenuated by the light on the water, which illuminates the whole work. The blacks are deep, warm, moving. The linework, to whose austere stiffness Buffet's composition owes its striking effect, is less stark, more mellow than usual. The beauty of this engraving, in addition to the composition, which is masterly in all Buffet's works, lies in the contrast between the fine, rich blacks and the light on the sea. The plate was printed in seventy-five copies in the Lacourière-Frélaut workshop in 1962.

The Steeple at Sauzon, 1962.
Drypoint, 50 × 65.3 cm, No. 17/75.
Published by Editions Lacourière, Paris.
Bibliography: Gerhard F. Reinz 275.
Private Collection.

Bernard Buffet

Biographies

PIERRE-AUGUSTE RENOIR

Pierre-Auguste Renoir

Born at Limoges on February 25, 1841; died at Cagnes-sur-Mer on December 17, 1919. When he was thirteen Renoir entered a Paris porcelain painter's workshop as an apprentice. At 21 he attended courses at the Ecole des Beaux-Arts and subsequently at Gleyre's. Made friends with Cézanne, Pissarro, Sisley, Monet, Bazille and Diaz. In 1873 Durand-Ruel, Caillebotte and Duret took an interest in his work. The Society of Painters, Engravers and Sculptors was founded in 1874, the year that saw the birth of Impressionism. There Renoir met all his friends. He did not take up engraving until he was fifty years old, first with two small soft-ground etchings after his painting *The Rustic Ball*, followed by an etching of a *Venus* for the frontispiece of Mallarmé's *Pages*. Most of his engravings were done after his own pictures. In 1892 he did his first lithograph, a portrait of his son Pierre. In 1894 he met Ambroise Vollard; in 1896 Auguste Clot, who played an important part in the production of Renoir's and Cézanne's color prints. Both artists were so preoccupied with painting that far too often they drew the designs for their lithographs on transfer paper and merely watercolored the first proof to show the printer the shades they wanted. Renoir was more interested in lithography than in engraving on copper and Vollard encouraged him to keep it up. The result was *The Pinned Hat, Twelve Lithographs, Mlle Dieterle*, portraits of Cézanne, Wagner and Rodin, and likenesses of his sons Jean and Claude. In about 1912 Renoir's rheumatism became aggravated to the point where he was forced to forgo engraving and tie a brush to his hand so as to be able to paint right up to the day of his death.

Bibliography: Galerie Arnold, *Ausstellung Graphischer Kunst*, Dresden 1913; L. Delteil, *Le Peintre-Graveur illustré. Renoir*, Vol. XVII, Paris 1923; *Catalogue XXᵉ Exposition des Peintres-Graveurs*, Bibl. Nat., Paris 1933; R. Cogniat and A. Vollard, *L'Œuvre gravé de Renoir*, Galerie des Beaux-Arts, Paris 1934; C. Roger-Marx, *La Gravure originale en France de Manet à nos Jours*, Hyperion, Paris 1939; M. Drucker, *Renoir*, Tisné, Paris 1944; C. Roger-Marx, *Les Lithographies de Renoir*, Sauret, Monte Carlo 1951; Serge Gauthier, *Catalogue, Hommage à Berthe Morisot et P.-A. Renoir*, Limoges Museum 1952; J. Laran, *L'Estampe*, Vols. I and II, Paris 1959; Adhémar, Hebert and Angebault, *Les plus belles Gravures du Monde occidental, 1410-1914*, Bibl. Nat., Paris 1966.

PAUL GAUGUIN

Paul Gauguin

Born in Paris on June 7, 1848; died at Fatui Iwa (Marquesa Islands) on May 8, 1903. In 1851 the Gauguins, fearing the future Napoleon III, settled in Lima, Peru. On returning to France in 1863, Gauguin entered the Navy. In 1871 he had a good financial position as a stockbroker's clerk. In 1873 he married a Danish girl and started to draw. In 1876 his work was accepted by the Salon. He took part in the Impressionist exhibitions. He left the Stock Exchange, abandoned his wife and family and suffered penury. In 1889 he did his first engravings: eleven zincographs printed by Ancourt. In 1891 he did his only etching, a portrait of Mallarmé. In 1894 he did another zincograph and his only lithograph, *Manao Tupapau*. About that time he took up wood engraving (using end wood first and side wood later) in France after his first voyage to Tahiti. From then on he used no other medium and produced fifty-five woodcuts, twelve of them for the titles of his diary in Tahiti, entitled *Le Sourire*. So Gauguin produced about seventy prints in all.

Bibliography: M. Guérin, *Œuvre gravé de Gauguin*, Floury, Paris 1927; H.-M. Petiet, *Catalogue de l'Exposition des Gravures de Gauguin*, Galerie de la Pléiade, Paris 1931; G. Daragnès, *Les Bois gravés de Gauguin*, A.M.G., Paris 1935; R. S. Field, *Gauguin's Noa Noa*, in The Burlington Magazine, London, September 1968.

Aristide Maillol
Photo G. Karquel

ARISTIDE MAILLOL

Born at Banyuls on December 8, 1861; died there on September 24, 1944. Decided to become a painter and in 1882 won a scholarship to the Ecole des Beaux-Arts in Paris. Expelled. Made friends with the Nabis, particularly with Maurice Denis. In 1884 he exhibited in the Salon des Indépendants. In 1893 he opened a tapestry workshop at Banyuls, choosing the woolen yarns himself and the plants for the dyes, which were exclusively vegetable. An eye malady forced him to give up tapestry making. In 1894 he met Gauguin in Brussels. Acting on his example, he produced pottery and wood sculpture. At the age of forty he devoted himself entirely to sculpture. He was also a great draughtsman and illustrator. He went in for high quality, handmade paper and, with the assistance of Count Kessler, set up a paper mill at Monval. He executed woodcuts for Virgil's *Eclogues* (1926) and Longus's *Daphnis and Chloe* (1937); lithographs for Verhaeren's *Belle Chair* (1931) and his masterpiece Ovid's *Art of Love* (1935); etchings for Ronsard's *Livre des Folastreries* (1940). From 1924 on he produced lithographs on separate sheets for the publisher E. Frapier. Maillol died from injuries sustained in a motorcar accident on his way to visit Raoul Dufy. He was almost eighty-three.

Bibliography: M. Lafargue, *Maillol Sculpteur et Lithographe*, Paris 1925; J. Cladel, *Maillol*, Paris 1937; J. Rewald, *Catalogue des Bois de Maillol*, New York 1945; J. Rewald, "Maillol Illustrateur" in *Portique*, 1, Paris 1945; Marcel Guérin, *L'Œuvre gravé de Maillol*, Paris 1948; P. Camo, *Maillol, mon Ami*, Henri Kaeser, Lausanne 1950.

Paul Signac

PAUL SIGNAC

Born in Paris on November 11, 1863; died there on August 15, 1935. When only 17 years old he was so impressed by a show of Claude Monet's work that he started painting in the open air after the manner of the Impressionists. In 1884 he was one of the founders of the Salon des Indépendants, where he met Seurat. Between them they invented Neo-Impressionism. They were joined by Camille Pissarro, H. E. Cross and Maximilien Luce. Signac became an ardent propagandist of his pictorial and sociological ideas. In 1899 he wrote a work of capital importance entitled *From Eugène Delacroix to Neo-Impressionism*. Signac was not only a painter but also a sailor. He owned several yachts in which he made a great many cruises. From his favorite ports he brought back some wonderful watercolors that served him as sketches for oils in his studio. In 1895 or thereabouts Signac met Vollard and at Clot's did a dozen color lithographs in the same pointillist style he employed in his paintings. He also did a few soft-grounds and etchings, some of which are still entirely unknown. The relative copper and zinc plates are deposited with a copperplate printer in Paris. As a man Signac was spirited and liberal. As a man of letters he was passionately interested in science. He loved life intensely.

Bibliography: L. Couturier, *Signac*, Crès, Paris 1922; C. Roger-Marx, *Signac*, Vienna 1921; G. Besson, *Signac, Dessins*, Braun, Paris 1950; C. Roger-Marx, *La Gravure originale au XIXe Siècle*, Somogy, Paris 1962.

Edvard Munch

EDVARD MUNCH

Born at Løten (Norway) on December 12, 1863; died at Ekely, near Oslo, on January 25, 1944. The son of a panel doctor. His childhood was marked by the sickness and death of his mother and two of his sisters. After studying at Oslo, he traveled for twenty years: Paris, the South of France, Italy, Germany. Associated with *avant-garde* writers and painters. In 1883, on his first stay in Paris, he was influenced by the Impressionists. In 1890, during his second stay, by the Post-Impressionists. In 1895 he executed engravings in Clot's Paris workshop. That was an important landmark in his graphic work, which is more significant than his painting. The year before he had taken up etching in Berlin. Now, with the same speed, he produced at Clot's his first lithographs and woodcuts, which were masterworks. Munch employed many different techniques in the eight hundred prints that make up his graphic *œuvre*. The great Expressionist was obsessed by life—he wanted his painting to be a "Frieze of Life"—and the themes that preoccupied him most were love and death. He had been far too close to the latter during his childhood and it was responsible for his dreadful fear of malancholy and solitude. Love, in his eyes, was a terrible evil force; the triumph of woman over man. He took the same view of it as his friend Strindberg and did not hesitate to represent it as a vampire.

Bibliography: G. Schiefler, *Verzeichnis des graphischen Werks E. Munchs bis 1906*, Vol. I, B. Cassirer, Berlin 1907; G. Schiefler, *E. Munch, Das graphische Werk 1906–1926*, Euphorium, Berlin 1928; Pola Gauguin, *Grafikeren. E. Munch*, I, II, Oslo 1945–6; S. Willoch, *The Etchings of E. Munch*, G. Tanum, Oslo 1950; O. Sarvig, *E. Munch grafik*, Gyldendal, Copenhagen 1964; P. Hougen, *E. Munch. Œuvre graphique*, Musée des Arts décoratifs, Paris and Tours, Nice, Cannes, Avignon, St-Etienne, Bordeaux, Orléans, 1969; W. S. Lieberman and E. Feinblatt, *E. Munch Lithographs, Etchings, Woodcuts*, Los Angeles County Museum of Art, 1969.

Henri de Toulouse-Lautrec

HENRI DE TOULOUSE-LAUTREC

Born at Albi on November 24, 1864; died at Malromé Castle on September 9, 1901. This scion of a very old noble family descended from the Albigensian Catharists, this legendary bohemian, always remained an aristocrat both as a man and as an artist. Crippled beyond hope by two accidents, he sought escape in art but nobly insisted on being treated as a normal man. He had loved drawing from his earliest childhood and with René Princetau's help discovered painting. In 1881 he took his final high-school examinations and the following year studied painting under Léon Bonnat and later under Fernand Cormon. Was strongly influenced by Van Gogh. In 1886 started out on his own. Médrano's circus, Bruant's music-hall, the Moulin de la Galette. Made friends with Pissarro, Degas, Gauguin, Seurat. In 1891 he did his first lithograph: a poster for the Moulin-Rouge. Continued to work in that medium until the year before he died. His most productive years were 1894 (fifty-four lithographs) an 1895 (seventy-eight lithographs). In 1898 he tried his hand at drypoint on zinc, executing nine plates in that medium, and also did forty lithographs. Lautrec, an extraordinary draughtsman, was one of those great painters in whose *œuvre* engraving occupies an important place and sometimes resulted in works of far greater significance than their paintings.

Bibliography: L. Delteil, *Le Peintre-Graveur illustré*, Vols. X and XI, Paris 1920; W. Rotzler, *Les Affiches de Toulouse-Lautrec*, Holbein, Basle 1946; C. Roger-Marx, *Les Lithographies de Toulouse-Lautrec*, Hazan, Paris 1948; E. Julien, *Les Affiches de Toulouse-Lautrec*, Sauret, Monte Carlo 1950; J. Adhémar, *Œuvre graphique de Toulouse-Lautrec*, Bibl. Nat., Paris 1951; J. Lassaigne, *Lautrec*, Skira, Geneva 1953; M. Lecomte, *Lithographies de Toulouse-Lautrec*, collection Maurice Loncle, Galerie Charpentier sale, Paris 1959; P. Huisman and G. Dortu, *Lautrec par Lautrec*, Edita, Lausanne 1964; J. Adhémar, *Toulouse-Lautrec, Lithographies, Pointes-sèches, Œuvre complet*, A.M.G., Paris 1965; Fermigier, *Toulouse-Lautrec*, Pall Mall Press, London and New York 1969; F. Novotny, *Toulouse-Lautrec*, Phaidon Press, London and New York 1969; *Unpublished Correspondence of Toulouse-Lautrec*, Phaidon Press, London and New York 1969.

SUZANNE VALADON

Born at Bessines-sur-Gartempe on September 23, 1865; died in Paris on April 6, 1938. Arriving in Paris when still very young, she started as a performer on the flying trapeze and later associated with artists in the Lapin Agile tavern on Montmartre. At eighteen she had a son, Maurice, who took the name Utrillo. She worked as a model for Renoir, Toulouse-Lautrec, Steinlen, Puvis de Chavannes. But she was a model who took an interest in art: in fact, she had been fond of drawing even as a child. Degas, who admired her "strong, supple line," advised her to take up engraving. It was under his guidance

Suzanne Valadon

that she did her first print in 1895, a soft-ground etching entitled *Nude at Her Toilet*. Like Degas, she pulled the first proofs herself. Her handling of this medium revolutionized a technique that had degenerated into flaccidity. She treated her zinc plates like a sculptor, biting them deep with a strong acid. Her subject matter varied little: mothers tending their children; women washing themselves; servant girls bustling about. Her harsh prints have no trace of gentleness; they show us the bodies of thin children who have grown too fast, of women deformed by age or work. In a single year she engraved twelve zinc plates. Then, in 1904 and 1905, she reverted to the drypoint and again from 1908 to 1910. Suzanne Valadon's graphic *œuvre* is not very numerous, but, like all great draughtsmen, she impresses us by the masterly firmness of her line.

Bibliography: C. Rey, Preface to Catalogue: *Dessins et Gravures de S. Valadon*, Galerie Bernier, Paris 1929; C. Roger-Marx, *Dix-huit Planches originales de S. Valadon (1895–1910)* with a catalogue essay, Daragnès, Paris 1932; C. Roger-Marx, *La Gravure originale en France de Manet à nos Jours*, Hyperion, Paris 1939; N. Jacometti, *S. Valadon*, Geneva 1947; R. Beachboard, *La Trinité maudite*, Amiot-Dumont, Paris 1952.

Pierre Bonnard

PIERRE BONNARD

Born at Fontenay-aux-Roses on October 3, 1867; died at Le Cannet on January 23, 1947. Obtained a law degree after a serious course of study, but in 1888 took up drawing at the Académie Julian. First attracted attention with a lithograph, the poster for France-Champagne, printed by Ancourt in 1889. From 1892 to 1895 he lithographed separate color prints and did the illustrations for his brother-in-law Claude Terrasse's *Petites Scènes familières* in black and white and for *Escarmouche* in bister black. These were followed by the poster for *La Revue Blanche* and the lithographs for that album. Then came his meeting with André Mellerio, for whom he lithographed a poster and the illustrations for his *Lithographie en Couleurs*. Vollard took him to Clot's workshop, where he executed the masterly color prints whose value his contemporaries failed to grasp. It took all the persistence of the publisher E. Frapier to persuade the artist to revert to lithography in 1924, this time in black and white. Bonnard was a great illustrator. Thanks to him Longus's *Daphnis and Chloé* and, still more, Verlaine's *Parallèlement* deserve a place among the finest books of all time. His graphic *œuvre* comprises four hundred and forteen lithographs and eighty less successful etchings executed for Mirbeau's *Dingo* and Vollard's *Sainte Monique*.

Bibliography: J. Floury, "Catalogue de l'Œuvre gravé", in *Bonnard* by C. Terrasse, Paris 1923; C. Roger-Marx, "Bonnard Illustrateur de La Fontaine" in *Portique*, 5, Paris 1947; L. Werth, "Bonnard Illustrateur" in *Portique*, 7, Paris 1950; T. Natanson, *Le Bonnard que je propose*, Cailler, Geneva 1952; C. Roger-Marx, *Bonnard Lithographe*, Sauret, Monte Carlo 1952; E. Rouir, "Quelques Remarques sur les Lithographies de P. Bonnard" in *Le Livre et l'Estampe*, 53–54, 1968.

KER XAVIER ROUSSEL

Born at Lorry-lès-Metz on December 10, 1867; died at L'Etang-la-Ville on June 5, 1944. As a pupil of the Lycée Condorcet in Paris, made friends with Maurice Denis and Edouard Vuillard. Together with the latter, worked in Maillard's studio and later at the Académie Julian, where he met Bonnard and Sérusier. In 1889, as one of the Nabis, he exhibited in the Café Volpini and at Le Barc de Bouteville's. Roussel first approached engraving through lithography in 1892. He continued to work in that medium during the years that followed and by 1943, the date of his last print, has produced ninety-four lithographs both in color and in black and white. If we add the thirty-one lithographs he did to illustrate Virgil's *Bucolics*, the total reaches one hundred and twenty-five. It was only later that he took up copper engraving, though less intensively. His first plates date from 1914, but it was chiefly after World War I, starting in 1920, that he did etchings, aquatints and soft grounds: some thirty plates in all. This means that Ker Xavier Roussel executed a total

Ker Xavier Roussel

of some one hundred and fifty prints. Most of them display a rustic charm and are flooded with light. They do not yet attract the interest they deserve and cannot fail to be greatly sought after when their elegance and beauty is finally grasped by an ignorant public.

Bibliography: L. Werth, *K. X. Roussel*, Paris 1931; D. Günter Busch and H. Helms, *Gemälde, Handzeichnungen, Druckgraphik* (Salomon Collection), Kunsthalle Bremen 1965; J. Salomon, *K.X. Roussel* (with an original lithograph), La Bibliothèque des Arts, Paris 1967; J. Salomon, *Œuvre gravé de K.X. Roussel*, Mercure de France, Paris 1968.

Edouard Vuillard

EDOUARD VUILLARD

Born at Cuiseaux on November 11, 1868; died at La Baule on June 21, 1940. His family were small textile manufacturers and he always kept a taste for draped interiors. He studied seriously at the Lycée Condorcet with Maurice Denis and K.X. Roussel. The latter became his brother-in-law and encouraged him to take up painting. At the Académie Julian he met Bonnard. In 1889 a charcoal drawing opened the doors of the Society of French Artists. In 1892 he took up lithography in Ancourt's workshop. Of his sixty-seven prints sixty are lithographs, of which twenty-six are in color, and seven are etchings. It was Vollard who urged him to do his finest color lithographs—*The Tuileries Gardens, Children at Play* and the twelve plates plus a frontispiece for *Paysages et Intérieurs*. In 1898 he did the first of his seven etchings, a portrait of the painter Van Rysselberghe. In 1937 he executed four etchings of the Square Vintimille, of which one is very fine indeed, for *Paris 1937*. In 1935, together with Segonzac and Villebœuf, he illustrated *117 Recettes de Cuisine* for Henry-Jean Laroche, contributing six very fine lithographs in black and white. This makes it all the more regrettable that Vollard, discouraged by the indifference with which the handsome books he published with illustrations by Bonnard were received, gave up the idea of having Vuillard illustrate Mallarmé's *Hérodiade*.

Bibliography: Henri Marguery, "Essai d'un Catalogue des Lithographies de Vuillard" in *L'Amateur d'Estampes*, Paris 1934; C. Roger-Marx, *Les Lithographies de Vuillard*, A.M.G., Paris 1934; C. Roger-Marx, *L'Œuvre gravé de Vuillard*, Sauret, Monte Carlo 1948.

Henri Matisse

HENRI MATISSE

Born at Cateau-Cambrésis on December 31, 1869; died at Cimiez, near Nice, on November 3, 1954. His mother was a gifted amateur painter. After high school he became a lawyer's clerk. An illness opened his eyes to art. Studied painting at night school, later at the Académie Julian and in Gustave Moreau's studio, where he met Marquet. Like Daumier, they followed Moreau's advice and sought their subjects in the streets. That simplified their linework, reducing it to the bare essentials. Matisse started to etch about 1903. In 1906 he did some woodcuts and lithographs. It is in the latter medium that he produced his masterworks from 1924 on. Some of his lithographs are very highly finished with fine light effects; others are line drawings. He also did linocuts. All in all, his graphic *œuvre* totals over five hundred sheets. He illustrated Mallarmé's *Poems* with twenty-nine etchings (1932), Montherlant's *Pasiphaé* with eighteen gouge engravings (1944) and Ronsard's *Les Amours* with one hundred and twenty lithographs (1948).

Bibliography: C. Roger-Marx, *Matisse*, A.M.G., 34, Paris 1933; *H. Matisse, Lithographies rares*, Catalogue Berggruen, Paris 1954; W. S. Liebermann, *Etchings by Matisse*, New York 1955; W. S. Liebermann, *Matisse. Fifty Years of his Graphic Art*, New York 1956.

Maurice Denis
Photo Roger-Viollet

MAURICE DENIS

Born at Granville on November 25, 1870; died as the result of an accident at Saint-Germain-en-Laye on November 13, 1945. Studied at the famous Académie Julian with

Sérusier. Was the spiritual leader of the Nabis. His first lithograph, which dates from 1889, had a religious theme. In 1890 his friendship with Gauguin led him to take up zincography, but he soon reverted to lithography, the medium he used for the vast majority of his prints. His graphic *œuvre* comprises one hundred and five lithographs in black and white and in color and a hundred for book illustration—thirty-one for André Gide's *Le Voyage d'Urien* (1893) and sixty-nine for Thompson's *Poems* commissioned by Ambroise Vollard and published by his brother in 1942. He also did nineteen woodcuts and four etchings (the first in 1905). The wood engraver Jacques Beltrand proved a magnificent interpreter of Denis' drawings, watercolors, lithographs and woodcuts for the purpose of book illustration. But of course these interpretative engravings, however fine, cannot be ascribed to Denis.

Bibliography: M. Brillant, *M. Denis, Peintre et Lithographe*, Paris 1926; J. Guignard, "Les Livres illustrés par M. Denis, Catalogue" in *Portique*, 4, Paris 1946; P. Cailler, *Catalogue raisonné de l'Œuvre gravé de M. Denis*, Cailler, Geneva 1968.

Georges Rouault
Photo Y. Chevallier

GEORGES ROUAULT

Born in Paris on May 27, 1871; died there on February 13, 1958. His father was a cabinet maker and his aunts were painters on porcelain. At the age of fourteen he was apprenticed to a glass painter and initiated in stained-glass window making. This environment gave him the craftsmanly integrity that he preserved all his life long. In 1890 he was admitted to the Ecole des Beaux-Arts, where he worked under Elie Delaunay and later under Gustave Moreau. His two entries for the Prix de Rome were both refused. In 1904 he met Léon Bloy and painted clowns, prostitutes and judges. In 1907 he met Vollard. In 1911 he stayed at Versailles, where he renewed his acquaintance with the Maritains and met André Suarès. In 1913 Vollard bought up his studio and in 1917 became his sole dealer. From 1917 to 1927 he was commissioned by Vollard to illustrate books: 1918, *Les Réincarnations du Père Ubu*, twenty-two etchings and aquatints in black and white; *Miserere*, fifty-eight etchings and aquatints in black and white; *Les Fleurs du Mal I*, fourteen aquatints in black and white. From 1924 to 1935 the publisher E. Frapier commissioned him to execute lithographs: *Circus Rider, Prostitute, Clown, Circus, Trio, White Horse, Christ on the Cross; Souvenirs intimes*, with his famous self-portrait. Between 1927 and 1933 he did lithographs of the heads of St. John and Verlaine and *Autumn* for Vollard. In 1930–8, also for Vollard, some extraordinary color aquatints: *Christ on the Cross, Autumn, Les Fleurs du Mal III, Circus, Passion* by A. Suarès and *The Circus of the Shooting Star*. All in all, Rouault's graphic *œuvre* comprises over three hundred and fifty works, of which about a hundred were never finished and were destroyed: some sixty lithographs in black and white, two or three in color, and almost two hundred copper engravings in color and in black and white. Rouault did not produce any woodcuts.

Bibliography: J. Maritain, *G. Rouault Peintre et Graveur*, Paris 1926; C. Roger-Marx, *L'Œuvre gravé de Rouault*, Byblis 1931, N. Wheeler, "The Prints of Rouault" in *Art News*, Oct. 8, 1938; Abbé Morel, "Le Miserere de G. Rouault" in *L'Etoile Filante*, Le Seuil, Paris 1951; *Rouault, Peintures, Gouaches, Miserere*, Exhib. Albi 1956; P. Courthion, *Rouault*, Flammarion, Paris 1962; G. Marchiori, *G. Rouault*, Bibliothèque des Arts, Paris–Lausanne 1965; Kornfeld and Klipstein, *G. Rouault, Graphik und illustrierte Bücher*, Berne 1966.

Albert Marquet

ALBERT MARQUET

Born in Bordeaux on March 27, 1875; died in Paris on June 14, 1947. His childhood was saddened by poor health and by sickness that accentuated his shyness and made him a recluse all his life long. In 1890 he settled in Paris with his mother. Was admitted to the

Ecole des Arts Décoratifs, made friends with Matisse. In 1897 entered Gustave Moreau's class at the Ecole des Beaux-Arts. In 1900, to earn his living, worked with Matisse on the decoration of the Paris World Fair. Discovered Monet, Cézanne and Van Gogh. Though a precursor of the Fauves, he never viewed color as either an end in itself or as a means to let off steam. In 1907 he went to live on the Quai Saint-Michel in the same house as Matisse. His colors became bright and varied, his style quiet. Marquet had a wonderful gift for rendering light and space. Between 1910 and 1914 he did a number of splendid female nudes. Made several trips abroad. Took up engraving in 1928. Executed drypoints after the manner of Jongkind's etchings, besides woodcuts and lithographs. Illustrated his wife's book, *Images d'une Petite Ville arabe*, which was published in the year of her death, with twenty-six etchings, and *Séjour à Venise* by Charles de Brosses with thirty-one etchings, of which five were in color. Jean Cassou's *Rhapsodie parisienne* with fifteen lithographs by Marquet was published in 1950. Between 1930 and 1932 he did some very fine lithographs of seaports in black and white.

Bibliography: F. Fosca, *Marquet*, Paris 1922; F. Jourdain, *Marquet*, Paris 1933; G. Besson, *Introduction à l'Exposition Marquet*, Galerie Schmit, Paris 1967.

JACQUES VILLON (real name Gaston Duchamp)

Jacques Villon
Photo Roger Hauert

Born at Damville on July 31, 1875; died at Puteaux on June 9, 1963. His father was a notary public, his mother was the daughter of the engraver E. Nicolle. He did his first two copper engravings—a profile of his father and a portrait of his grandfather—when he was only sixteen. Gave up the study of law and, like all his brothers and sisters, devoted himself to art. In 1895 entered Cormon's studio. Was an admirer of Toulouse-Lautrec. Contributed drawings to various newspapers. Produced his first lithographs. In 1899 reverted to copper engraving and printed his first color aquatints in Delâtre's workshop on the Rue Tourlesque. Continued to work in this medium until 1909 though that did not prevent him from doing etchings and soft-grounds in black and white as well as lithographs, particularly for posters. In 1907 was deeply impressed by the Cézanne retrospective exhibition. Later Cubism made a strong impact on his art in general and his prints in particular. He invented his own brand of Cubism. In 1912, the Section d'Or exhibition was held. Villon's finest prints are drypoints executed between 1911 and 1913. It was not till 1920 that he reverted to engraving to make reproductions—the only valid ones executed during this century—of paintings by contemporary artists in color aquatint. Though he continued to work along these lines until 1930, he also produced original prints, such as *The Chess Board*. After 1930 he felt free to engrave as his inspiration dictated. Though he always remained loyal to Cubism, he took his cue from real life and created figures and objects in accordance with his own personal vision. In these works he solved the permanent problem of light with a mastery that is truly amazing. Always modest in the extreme, he only became famous when he was seventy years old. Today he is considered one of the five greatest engravers of the twentieth century.

Bibliography: Catalogue Bernheim-Jeune, Etats des Gravures en Couleurs de Reproduction d'après les Maîtres modernes, Paris 1928; J. Auberty and C. Pérussaux, *Catalogue de l'Œuvre gravé de Villon*, Prouté, Paris 1950; W. Lieberman, *Jacques Villon, His Graphic Art*, Museum of Modern Art 1953; J. Adhémar, *Catalogue de l'Exposition de l'Œuvre gravé, Préface*, Galerie Louis Carré, Paris 1954; Mellquist, "Biographie" in *Art-Documents* (reprint, Exhibition of Jacques Villon's graphic art, Musée Rath), Geneva 1955; J. Askeland, *Jacques Villon grafiske Arbeuder*, Royal Library Copenhagen 1957; J. Adhémar, *Catalogue de l'Œuvre gravé de Jacques Villon*, Bibl. Nat., Paris 1959; A. Wick, *Jacques Villon, Master of Graphic Art*, Exhibition in Museum of Fine Arts, Boston 1964.

Maurice de Vlaminck

MAURICE DE VLAMINCK

Born in Paris on April 4, 1875; died at Rueil-la-Gadelière on October 1, 1958. His father was a violin teacher of Flemish origin; his mother taught the piano. His first job was as an apprentice mechanic. In 1893 he became a racing cyclist. In 1896 played the violin in restaurants and popular dance halls. He also wrote articles for anarchist newspapers. "I hate the smell of museums, their stiffness, their monotony. I hate the word 'classic.' Science gives me the toothache," he was fond of saying. He detested everything that restricted a man's personality. In 1899 he met Derain, with whom he shared a studio at Chatou. To earn his living, he wrote books. In 1901, the Van Gogh exhibition was held. In 1905 he was introduced by Derain to Matisse. In 1906 Vollard bought up all the pictures in his studio. He became one of the founders of Fauvism. His first woodcuts—all in black and white—date from about 1907. Though they differ from those of Gauguin and Munch, they have their origin in them; the influence of Van Gogh is seen in both. In 1921 he did his first lithographs. In 1924 the publisher Frapier commissioned many lithographs, etchings and drypoints. Vlaminck employed these media to illustrate a dozen books. All in all his graphic *œuvre* comprises over two hundred and thirty works—about one hundred woodcuts, the same number of lithographs, of which two or three in color, and some thirty etchings, drypoints and aquatints.

Bibliography: F. Carco, *Vlaminck*, Paris 1921; L. Werth, *Vlaminck, Peintre-Graveur*, Paris 1928; J.-C. Romand, *Vlaminck, Œuvre gravé* (Catalogue Exhibition Galerie Sagot-Le Garrec), Paris 1956; J. Frapier, *Galerie des Peintres-Graveurs, Catalogue No. 4*, 1964.

Raoul Dufy

RAOUL DUFY

Born at Le Havre on June 3, 1877; died at Forcalquier (Haute-Provence) on March 23, 1953. His father was fond of playing the organ; his eight brothers and sisters were nearly all musicians. At fourteen he became a shop assistant but attended night classes at the Ecole des Beaux-Arts of Le Havre with Othon Friesz. In 1900 he won a scholarship to the Ecole des Beaux-Arts in Paris, where he worked under Léon Bonnat. From 1901 to 1904 he was influenced by the Impressionists and Lautrec; in 1905 by Matisse. In 1906 he joined the Fauves and made friends with Marquet. In 1908 he went with Braque to L'Estaque. In 1909 he met Paul Poiret, who gave him the money to set up a textile printing works for which he designed the patterns. In 1910 he met Guillaume Apollinaire and did his first prints—thirty-three woodcuts in black and white—for his *Bestiaire*. He took up lithography about 1924, first in black and white and later in color, using the medium first for book illustrations, as he had done with his woodcuts, and subsequently for separate sheets. In 1928 he did his first etchings for the frontispieces of books. In 1929 Vollard asked him to illustrate *La Belle Enfant*, for which he did one hundred and ten etchings. In 1937 he executed one hundred color lithographs for *Les Aventures de Tartarin de Tarascon*. Dufy produced close on five hundred prints in all—one hundred and forty-five woodcuts, over one hundred and sixty lithographs and some hundred and sixty etchings. The vast majority served to illustrate books.

Bibliography: C. Roger-Marx, "Dufy Illustrateur" in *Renaissance*, No. 3, pp. 40–42, Paris 1938; P. Camo, "Dans l'Atelier de Dufy, Bibliographie des *Ouvrages illustrés*" in *Portique*, 4, 1946; P. Courthion, *R. Dufy*, Cailler, Geneva 1951; N. Rauch, *Les Peintres et le Livre, 1867–1957*, Geneva 1957.

Emile Laboureur
Photo Manuel

ÉMILE LABOUREUR (assumed the Christian name Jean-Emile in 1903)

Born at Nantes on August 16, 1877; died at Kerfahler on June 16, 1943. While still at school, he decorated his copybooks with careful colored drawings. At the age of eighteen, went to Paris, where Lotz-Brissonneau introduced him to Auguste Lepère. In 1896 he did his first woodcuts and etchings. In 1897 he met Toulouse-Lautrec, who initiated him in lithography. In 1899 he studied the German engravers in the print rooms in Berlin, Kassel, Frankfurt and Munich. In 1903 he went to America, where he did drawings, gouaches and engravings. Traveled in France, the United States, Canada, England. Visited Paris, Corsica, Naples, Athens, Constantinople, Smyrna, Ephesus, Florence, Nantes, and returned to Paris. In 1909 Lotz-Brissonneau established the titles for his engravings. 1911–13, first one-man shows. In 1913 *The Amazons* was an important landmark in his art. During World War I he was engaged as an interpreter by the Allied armies. Met Gromaire. 1916, first copper engravings. In 1918 renewed contact with Dufy, Segonzac and Marie Laurencin. From 1920 to 1935, his heyday; he lived in Paris or in Brittany. Bursting with energy, he wrote newspaper articles, founded the Society of Independent Painter-Engravers (1923) and busied himself with the Society for Original Wood Engraving. In 1921 he did his first illustrations for Giraudoux. In 1926 he illustrated that author's *Suzanne et le Pacifique*; in 1930 Toulet's *Contrerimes*; in 1931 *La Brière*. His graphic *œuvre* comprises close on a thousand copper engravings, three hundred and eighty woodcuts and eighty-one lithographs.

Bibliography: A. Lotz-Brissonneau, *Eaux-fortes, Bois et Lithographies d'E. Laboureur*, Paris 1909; M. Laurencin, *Cahier de l'Œuvre gravé par Laboureur* (typescript), Cabinet des Estampes, 1928; L. Godefroy, *L'Œuvre gravé de Laboureur*, Vol. 1, Paris 1929; J. Prinet, "Les Illustrations de J.-E. Laboureur" in *Portique*, 1, 1945; J. Loyer, *L'Œuvre gravé de Laboureur* (Sequel to Godefroy Vol. 1), Tournon, M. Lecomte, Paris.

JEAN FRÉLAUT

Born at Grenoble on July 17, 1879; died at Vannes on December 22, 1954. Frélaut's parents came from Brittany and he went with them to Vannes when his father, a General, retired there in 1889. In 1897, on finishing high-school, entered the Ecole des Arts Décoratifs in Paris. Worked for five years in Cormon's studio. In 1903 Marcel Bertrand initiated him in drypoint and etching. Received advice from the engraver D. S. MacLaughlen. Bought a press and pulled his own prints. In 1905 he studied Rembrandt and Breugel in Holland. In 1920 retired to Vannes. His graphic *œuvre* comprises close on fifteen hundred works, mostly etchings and drypoints, a few woodcuts and twenty-six lithographs executed between 1925 and 1928. In 1934 was awarded the Prize for Engraving at the Venice Biennale. In 1938 took up book illustration. He illustrated fourteen books, among them a splendid edition of La Fontaine's *Fables* and the delightful *Ballades, Rondeaux et Complaintes* of Charles d'Orléans. Frélaut also did three hundred and fifty paintings in oils besides a great many watercolors and wash drawings as preliminaries for his engravings.

Jean Frélaut

Bibliography: L. Delteil, *Le Peintre-Graveur illustré, Frélaut*, Vol. XXXI, Paris 1926; J. Lethève, *J. Frélaut*, Catalogue of exhibition in the National Library, Paris 1955; M. Ferry, *J. Frélaut*, Catalogue of exhibition in the National Library at Nice, preface by Dunoyer de Segonzac, Nice 1957; H. de Parcevaux, Catalogue of exhibition in the Limur Museum, Vannes 1958; P. Cailler, *Sequel to Delteil* (not yet published), Geneva.

ANDRÉ DERAIN

Born at Chatou on June 18, 1880; died at Garches on September 10, 1954. A studious, intelligent youth, he prepared to enter the Ecole Centrale in Paris but preferred to devote himself to painting. When a pupil at the Académie Carrière, he met Matisse. In 1899 he made friends with Vlaminck. In 1905 the three young artists founded Fauvism. Derain was one of the first painters to admire Negro art and was captivated by Cubism, but thanks to his classical culture he was always influenced by the Old Masters. In 1906 he

André Derain

Pablo Picasso

produced his first etchings, a few female nudes, and his first woodcuts, friezes with human figures. These latter caught the eye of Kahnweiler, who commissioned a first book from him with thirty-two woodcuts in 1909. At that time Derain and Dufy, as disciples of Gauguin, were the leading lights of the new school of wood engravers. As such they renovated book illustration. Derain's first lithographs date from 1919; they were done to illustrate Vlaminck's *A la Santé du Corps*. In 1929 he did forty lithographs for Muselli's *Les Travaux et les Jeux*; in 1934, thirty-four line engravings for Vollard's edition of the *Satyricon* by Petronius Arbiter; in 1938, fifteen etchings for Ovid's *Heroides*. In 1940–2, one hundred and twenty-eight color woodcuts for Rabelais's *Pantagruel*. All in all, Derain's graphic *œuvre* comprises sixty-four etchings, forty-seven line engravings, seventeen drypoints, two hundred and fifty lithographs and two hundred and sixty-five woodcuts in black and white or in color—a total of some six hundred and fifty plates.

Bibliography: A. Gabory, *A. Derain, Lithographe, Xylographe, Aquafortiste*, A.M.G., pp. 119–26, Paris January 1931; J. Adhémar, Catalogue of Derain Exhibition, Bibl. Nat., Paris 1955; N. Rauch, *Les Peintres et le Livre*, Catalogue No. 6, Geneva 1957; J. Hugues, 50 *Ans d'Edition de D. H. Kahnweiler*, Galerie Louise Leiris, Paris 1958.

PABLO PICASSO (Pablo Ruiz Blasco)

Born at Malaga on October 25, 1881. Received his first drawing lessons from his father, a drawing teacher, at La Coruña in 1891. In 1895 the family moved to Barcelona, where young Pablo brilliantly passed the entry examination to the famous La Llonga art school. In 1897 exhibited drawings in a café called Els Quatre Gats and in Madrid. In 1899, in Barcelona, met Jaime Sabartès and did his first etching—*El Zurdo*. The following year saw him in Paris for the first time, where he did drawings. In 1901 did drawings in Madrid and Paris. Started to sign his works Picasso, which was his mother's maiden name. In 1904 settled definitively in Paris, where he rented a studio in the "Bateau Lavoir" and engraved *The Frugal Meal*. In 1905 he engraved *Les Saltimbanques*. In 1906 did drypoints on celluloid and his first woodcuts. From 1909 to 1915 produced Cubist prints. From 1916 to 1920 did neoclassic, Ingresque etchings. 1919 was the year of his first lithographs. In 1927 he did etchings for Balzac's *Le Chef-d'œuvre inconnu*; in 1930 etchings for Ovid's *Metamorphoses*. In 1933 started work on a set of one hundred copperplates for Vollard (the *Vollard Series*). In 1934 did *Lysistrata* and in 1935 the *Minotauromachy*. In 1937 painted *Guernica*, engraved *Franco's Dream and Lie*, the sugar aquatints for Buffon's *Histoire Naturelle*, and the portraits of Vollard that concluded the famous hundred-plate series. Picasso reverted to lithography in November 1945, producing his first color prints in that medium at Mourlot's. In 1948 he did *Gongora* and Reverdy's *Le Chant des Morts*. In 1949 the lithograph entitled *The Dove of Peace*. In 1950 the illustrations for Césaire's *Corps Perdu*. In 1952 the aquatint, *Woman at the Window*. From 1953 to 1957, aquatints, line engravings and lithographs (the *Jacqueline* series). In 1958 his first color linocuts. In 1959 the *Tauromachy* series and linocuts. From 1960 to 1967, aquatints, etchings, drypoints and line engravings. In 1968, from March 16 to October 5, three weeks before his 87th birthday, he did three hundred and fifty-seven etchings, line engravings, drypoints, mezzotints and aquatints.

Bibliography: B. Geiser, *Picasso, Peintre-Graveur*, Vol. I, 1899–1931, Berne 1933 and 1955; idem, Vol. II, 1932–4, Kornfeld and Klipstein, Berne 1968; Ch. Zervos, *Picasso, Peintures, Dessins, Gravures, de 1889 à 1932*, 7 vols. from 1943 to 1955; F. Mourlot, *Picasso Lithographe*, Vol. I, 1919–47, Vol. II, 1947–9, Vol. III, 1949–56, Vol. IV, 1956–63, A. Sauret, Monte Carlo 1949, 1950, 1956, 1964; Kahnweiler, *Picasso, Radierungen und Lithographien 1905–1952*, Prestel, Munich 1953; B. Geiser, *L'Œuvre gravé de Picasso, Introduction et Choix*, Clairefontaine, Lausanne 1955; J. Adhémar, *Picasso, Œuvre gravé*, Catalogue of first exhibition in Bibl. Nat., Paris 1955; *L'Œuvre gravé de P. Picasso*, Musée Rath, Geneva 1955; G. Bergengren, *Hommage à Picasso*, Malmö Museum 1956; H. Bolliger, *Pablo Picasso, Suite Vollard*, Niggli, Teufen (AR), Switzerland. Editions Parallèles, Paris 1956; M. Ferry, *Picasso, Œuvre gravé*, Catalogue Municipal Library Nice 1960; Galerie Louise Leiris, *45 Gravures sur Linoléum*, Paris 1960; Berggrüen, *Picasso, 60 Ans de Gravures*, Catalogue Paris 1964; J. Adhémar, Catalogue of second Exhibition of Graphic *Œuvre*, Bibl. Nat., Paris 1966; Louise Leiris, *Picasso 347 Gravures*, Paris 1968; *Œuvre gravé de Picasso*, Catalogue Kornfeld and Klipstein, Berne 1968.

Georges Braque
Photo Roger Hauert

GEORGES BRAQUE

Born at Argenteuil on May 13, 1882; died at Varengeville on August 31, 1963. The son of a house painter, Braque spent his childhood at Le Havre, where he attended the Ecole des Beaux-Arts. In 1902 he moved to Paris. In 1908, after being refused by the Salon d'Automne, he exhibited at Kahnweiler's. His first etching : a nude study. From 1910 to 1912 did Cubist etchings. On resuming print making in 1921, did his first lithograph— a still life in color. In that same year did his first woodcut. His next lithograph, in 1928, was in black and white. In 1931 did sixteen etchings with notes in the margins for Vollard's edition of Hesiod's *Theogony*. In 1932, a color lithograph entitled *Athénée* foreshadows the *Helios* suite of 1946. In 1934 he did two etchings, *Reclining Nude* and *The Dance*, after which he gave up that medium for several years. Braque's resumption of print making at Mourlot's in 1945, was marked by the production of color lithographs. From that year till his death in 1963 he did over a hundred and seventy-five lithographs, most of them in color. In 1949 he etched a bird on the wing, the first of a set of some twenty lithographs and etchnigs on that theme. After the *Theogony* Braque illustrated a number of important books, among them *Les Cinq Sapates* by F. Ponge, *Les Paroles transparentes* by Jean Paulhan, *La Liberté des Mers* by Pierre Reverdy, *Lettera Amorosa* by René Char.

Bibliography: J. Paulhan, *Braque, le Patron*, Mourlot, Paris 1945 and 2nd edition, Trois Collines, Geneva–Paris 1947; Braque, *Le Jour et la Nuit, Cahier de Georges Braque*, Gallimard, Paris 1952; *L'Œuvre graphique de Braque*, Musée des Beaux-Arts, Liège 1953; M. Seuphor, *Braque Graveur*, Catalogue Galerie Berggrüen, Paris 1953; *Das Graphische Œuvre von G. Braque*, Kunsthalle Basle 1954; P. Wember, *G. Braque, das Graphische Gesamtwerk 1907–1955*, illust. Catalogue Cologne, Bremen, Dusseldorf, Berlin 1955; E. Engelberts, *G. Braque, Œuvre graphique original*, Musée d'Art et d'Histoire and Galerie N. Rauch, Geneva 1958; R. Vieillard, *G. Braque, Grands Livres illustrés*, Maeght, Paris 1958; J. Adhémar and J. Lethève, *G. Braque, Œuvre graphique*, Bibl. Nat. Paris 1960; W. Hofmann, *L'Œuvre graphique de G. Braque*, Clairefontaine, Lausanne 1962; F. Mourlot, *Braque Lithographe, Catalogue complet*, Sauret, Monte Carlo 1963.

MAURICE UTRILLO

Born in Paris on December 26, 1883; died at Dax on November 5, 1955. Utrillo was born on the Butte Montmartre, the natural son of Suzanne Valadon, and was acknowledged in 1891 by Miguel Utrillo y Molins. At school the only subject in which he distinguished himself was mathematics. When still very young he formed habits of vagrancy and drinking, and underwent disintoxication treatment for the first time at Sainte-Anne, followed by a period of idleness. In 1902 a doctor advised his mother to teach him to paint in order to keep him busy. At the start he viewed it as a chore but soon took a fancy to it and revealed a surprisingly original talent. 1908–14 was his white period. He painted masterpieces by day and lived as a tramp and a drunk by night. Was interned at Picpus in 1919, in the Santé in 1921, again in Sainte-Anne, and lastly at Ivry. After 1909 he hardly ever painted from nature but only from picture postcards. His art refused to accept any theory or discipline but, strangely enough, was neither morbid nor immoral. His extraordinary gifts made him a builder, an architect and a colorist. In about 1924 he did eleven lithographs to illustrate an autobiographical text by his friend Francis Carco. His graphic *œuvre* comprises some twenty original lithographs, one of them in color.

Maurice Utrillo
Photo Facchetti

Bibliography: R. Rey, *Utrillo Peintre et Lithographe*, Paris 1925; R. Beachboard, *La Trinité maudite: Valadon, Utter, Utrillo*, Amiot-Dumont, Paris 1952; C. Roger-Marx, *Maurice Utrillo*, 1953; J. Frapier, *Galerie des Peintres-Graveurs, Catalogue No. II*, 1960, and *No. IV*, 1964.

André Dunoyer de Segonzac

ANDRÉ DUNOYER DE SEGONZAC

Born at Boussy-Saint-Antoine on July 7, 1884. Spent his childhood there and in Paris. Studied at the Lycées Louis-le-Grand and Henri IV. In 1900 drew the antiquities at the Ecole des Beaux-Arts as an independent pupil. In 1903 studied painting in Luc-Olivier Merson's private studio. In 1905 failed to obtain admission to the Ecole des Beaux-Arts. Returned to Merson, who sent him packing because he refused to obey instructions. Became a pupil of J.-P. Laurens. In 1908 went to Saint-Tropez for the first time, staying in Signac's villa "Les Cigales." Met Isadora Duncan, the dancer. In 1910, paintings— *The Village* and *Drinkers*. Exhibited at the Salon d'Automne. In 1912, Saint-Tropez and Italy. Took a studio at No. 13, Rue Bonaparte, where Derain lived. 1914–18, in the infantry, later in the camouflage section. 1919, at Chaville. First etchings for *Les Croix de Bois*. From 1923 to 1925 engraved *Fernande with Clasped Hands*, the *Suite Morin, Tableau de la Boxe*, a series on *Versailles* and the portrait of *Matéo Hernandez*. In 1925, bought "Le Maquis" at Saint-Tropez from the painter Charles Camoin. In 1928, engraved the *Farms with Threshing Floor* series. In 1928, the plates for *Bubu de Montparnasse*; in 1931, those for *La Treille Muscate* in Colette's house at Saint-Tropez. From 1930 to 1946, engraved the illustrations for Virgil's *Georgics* commissioned by Vollard. In 1935–6, did the *Beaches* and the *Joinville to Bougival* series. In 1937, first exhibition in the French National Library. Did engravings at Ville d'Avray. The *Georgics* were finished during World War II. From 1946 to 1950, engraved landscapes at Chaville and portraits. From 1951 to 1955, engraved at Bagatelle, Chaville and in the Vendôme district illustrations for *Quelques Sonnets de Ronsard*. In 1967 the largest show of his graphic work was organized in Blois Castle. His total graphic work comprises sixteen hundred sheets—a trial aquatint, a few lithographs and drypoints, the rest etchings. A few lines drawn by Segonzac on a copperplate suffice to render all the poetry of a landscape.

Bibliography: P. Jamot, *Dunoyer de Segonzac*, Fleury, Paris 1929; Exhibition Bibl. Nat., *Œuvre gravé de Dunoyer de Segonzac*, Paris 1937; C. Roger-Marx, *Dunoyer de Segonzac*, Cailler, Geneva 1951; A. Lioré and P. Cailler, *Catalogue de l'Œuvre gravé de Dunoyer de Segonzac, 1919–1927*, Vol. I, Cailler, Geneva 1958; Vol. II, *1928–1930*, Geneva 1959; Vol. III, *1930–1932*, Geneva 1963; Vol. IV, *1933–1935*, Geneva 1964; Vol. V, *1937–1947*, Geneva 1965; Vol. VI, *1948–1952*, Geneva 1966; Vol. VII, *1953–1956*, Geneva 1968; Vol. VIII not yet out; *Œuvre gravé de Dunoyer de Segonzac*, second exhibition Bibl. Nat., Paris 1958; G. Poisson, *Donation Dunoyer de Segonzac*, Musée de Sceaux, 1965; Roger Passeron, *Hommage à Dunoyer de Segonzac*, Château de Blois, 1967.

Marc Chagall

MARC CHAGALL

Born at Vitebsk (Russia) on July 7, 1887, of a large and very religious Jewish family. His childhood marked him for life and its memories still haunt his art. In 1907 he was apprenticed to a house painter and later to a photographer. Studied painting under an old teacher. Moved to St. Petersburg, where he worked with Léon Bakst and got the idea of going to Paris. In 1910 a wealthy patron paid for the trip. Rented a studio in "La Ruche" at Montparnasse, where he met Léger, Modigliani and Soutine. Studied the Old Masters in the Louvre. 1914–22, in Berlin and at Vitebsk; appointed Commissioner for Fine Arts by the Vitebsk Government. Back in Berlin, did the first engravings for *My Life*, his first lithographs and his first woodcuts. Returned to Paris in 1923. During the next four years did one hundred and seven plates for Gogol's *Dead Souls* commissioned by Vollard. In 1927 Vollard commissioned one hundred etchings for the *Fables* of La Fontaine and in 1931 one hundred and five etchings for *La Bible*. For the latter Chagall traveled in the Middle East. In 1941 he went to America, where he did thirteen color lithographs. In 1948 he returned definitively to France. In 1950 executed color lithographs in the Mourlot's workshop. In 1952 finished thirty-nine plates for *La Bible*, which had remained unfinished on Vollard's death. During the next ten years did a quantity of lithographs in color and in black and white, both as separate plates and for the *Verve Bible*. In 1961, forty-two lithographs for *Daphnis et Chloé*. In 1967 *The Circus*, twenty-three color lithographs plus seventeen in black and white. Chagall's graphic work, like his painting, has an extraordinary lyric freedom, a quality of weightlessness, and an absolutely original, unprecedented poetic spark.

Bibliography: P. Soupault, "Les Eaux-fortes de Chagall" in *Amour de l'Art*, Paris May 1926; J. Maritain, "Les Eaux-fortes de Chagall pour la Bible" in *Cahiers d'Art*, Paris 1934 (pp. 84–92); Ben Sussan, "Catalogue de l'Œuvre gravé de Chagall" in *Signature*, Nov. 1946; J. Lassaigne, "Chagall Gravures" in *Graphis*, 23, 1948; Galerie Gutekunst and Klipstein, *Chagall, Œuvre litho-graphié, 1950–1956*, Berne 1956; J. Adhémar and M. Sauvage, *Chagall, l'Œuvre gravé*, Bibl. Nat. Paris 1957; Franz Meyer, *Chagall, l'Œuvre gravé*, Hatje, Stuttgart 1957; F. Mourlot, *Chagall Litho-graphe 1922–1957*, Vol. I, Sauret, Monte Carlo 1960; *ibid. 1957–1962*, Vol. II, Sauret, Monte Carlo 1963.

Ossip Zadkine

OSSIP ZADKINE

Born at Smolensk (Russia) on July 15, 1890; died at Neuilly-sur-Seine on November 25, 1967. Did his first drawings at eight years of age and his first sculpture at twelve. In 1905 went to London, where his uncle took him to the Sunderland Art School. In 1909 entered the Ecole des Beaux-Arts in Paris. The tuition there repelled him so he went to live in "La Ruche." In 1912 moved to the Rue de Vaugirard. The following year a patron helped him to settle in the Rue Rousselet. Zadkine was the first, with Lipchitz, to adopt Cubism in sculpture. 1914, World War I. In 1917 Zadkine was gassed near Epernay and invalided out of the army. Did war drawings, which he used the following year for twenty-two etchings in a Cubist style of his own. They were his first engravings; he published them himself but could not sell them. No more engravings until 1928, when he did color etchings with lithographic or woodcut backgrounds. His first lithograph dates from 1948, after which he did one hundred and three, some in black and white, some in color. Zadkine's graphic *œuvre* comprises one hundred and eighty-three prints, of which eighty are etchings.

Bibliography: C. Czwiklitzer, *L'Œuvre gravé d'Ossip Zadkine*, Art. C.C. 1967; Galerie Motte, *O. Zadkine, Œuvre gravé*, Paris 1968.

MAX ERNST

Born at Brühl, near Cologne, on April 2, 1891; later granted French nationality. Entered Bonn University in 1909 and was greatly interested by the most recent works of Picasso, de Chirico and Macke. In 1914 met Hans Arp, a self-taught poet like himself, with whom he founded the Cologne branch of Dada in 1919. In 1921 moved to Paris, where he became one of the promoters of Surrealism. Rejecting discipline of any kind, he invented new techniques and in his paintings treated a number of different themes. In 1925 discovered frottage—it consists in rubbing with a lead pencil a sheet of paper laid over a textured surface (wood, fabric, leaf, or the like)—and utilized the process in lithography. In forty years Ernst illustrated over forty books, either with reproductions of collages or with genuine engravings, besides a score for which he did the frontispiece and a dozen he illustrated in collaboration with other artists. In 1939 he was twice interned with Hans Bellmer. The first time he was set free by Paul Eluard, the second by the Franco-German armistice of 1940. In 1941 he went to the United States, where he married Peggy Guggen-

Max Ernst
Photo Le Point Cardinal

Marcel Gromaire
Photo Willemin

heim the following year. The marriage ended in divorce and in 1946 he married Dorothea Tanning in Los Angeles. In 1954, the year of his consecration at the Venice Biennale, they settled at Huismes in the Loire Valley. Ernst's happiness at that time is visible in his works. At present he is living at Seillans in the Var Department.

Bibliography: A. Breton, *Les Pas perdus*, N.R.F., Paris 1924; A. Breton. *Le Surréalisme et la Peinture*, N.R.F., Paris 1928; M. Ernst, "Œuvres de 1919 à 1936" in *Cahiers d'Art*, Paris 1937; M. Ernst, *Beyond Painting*, Wittenborn Schultz Inc., New York 1948; M. Ernst, *Gemälde und Graphik 1920–1950*, Brühl Exhibition, 1951; Waldberg, *Max Ernst*, J.-J. Pauvert, Paris 1958; M. Jean, *Histoire de la Peinture surréaliste*, Le Seuil, Paris 1959; Pieyre de Mandiargues, "Le Renouveau dans la Carrière de M. Ernst" in *Figures*, 1. Sept. 1961, Paris and New York; R. von Holten, "Xylografisk besatthet, M. Ernsts Collageteknik" in *Imaginär Verklighet*, Stockholm 1962; Huges and Poupard-Lieussou, *M. Ernst, Ecrits et Œuvre gravé*, Bibl. Municipale, Tours, Point Cardinal, Paris 1963.

MARCEL GROMAIRE

Born at Noyelles-sur-Sambre on July 24, 1892. His father came from Lorraine, his mother was a Fleming. He studied first at Douai and later in Paris, at the Lycée Bouffon and the Law Faculty. After 1910 he frequented the studios of Colarossi, Ranson and La Palette in Montparnasse. Was influenced by Matisse's drawings. In 1913 he exhibited at the Salon des Indépendants. Called to the colors in 1914; wounded in 1916. In 1921 exhibited at the Salon d'Automne. In 1922 did his first etchings. In his eyes drawing comes first; color, no matter how exciting, is the handmaiden of form. He despises slackness, carelessness, disorder, imprecision. His drawings are that of an engraver and reveals a Cubist structure. Volume, rigor, firmness, force, are the typical qualities of his work. Gromaire has been a member of the Society of French Painter-Engravers since 1937. With Jean Lurçat he took an interest in tapestry : his cartoons display forceful composition expressed in a few sober colors. Gromaire's graphic *œuvre* totals some two hundred and fifty plates, including the woodcuts for *L'Homme de Troupe* (1918) and *Ruptures* (1925).

Bibliography: G. Pillement, *Gromaire*, Paris 1929; *Œuvre gravé de Gromaire*, Catalogue exhibition Galerie Carré, Paris 1956; J. Frapier, *Marcel Gromaire, Gravures, Dessins,* Catalogue exhibition Oslo, Trondhjem, Stavanger, Bergen, 1968–9; M. Avati, *Album des Peintres-Graveurs français, 80ᵉ Anniversaire*, Paris 1969.

JOAN MIRÓ

Born at Montroig near Barcelona on April 20, 1893. Admitted to the Academy of Fine Arts in Barcelona at the age of fourteen. In 1910 his parents made him give up painting for trade. In 1912 he returned to painting in the Gali Academy (Barcelona). First showed his work in 1918. In 1919 went to Paris for the first time, where he made friends with Picasso. Settled there in 1920. Joined the Dadaist movement. In 1921, first exhibition in Paris. In 1922, painted *The Farm*. In 1925 joined the Surrealists. In 1930 did his first lithographs for Tristan Tzara's *L'Arbre des Voyageurs*. In 1932–3, his first etching : *Childhood*. In 1938, his first drypoints, the black and red series, and his first linocut. In 1940 the war caused him to leave Paris for Majorca and then for Barcelona, where in 1944 he did the set of fifty lithographs in black and white entitled *Barcelona*. In that same year he returned to Paris and in 1947 went to America. From 1948 to 1950 he did seventy-two color lithographs for Tzara's *Parler seul*. In 1950, his first color woodcuts. In 1954, awarded the Graphic Art Prize at the Venice Biennale. In 1958 he finished his hundred color woodcuts for Eluard's *A toute Epreuve*. So far Miró has done over seven hundred prints in every medium

Joan Miró
Photo Roger Hauert

Bibliography: J. J. Sweeney, *J. Miró*, The Museum of Modern Art, New York 1941; G. Greenberg, *J. Miró*, The Quadrangle Press, New York; J. Prevert and Ribemont-Dessaignes, *Joan Miró*, Maeght, Paris 1956; J. Dupin, *Joan Miró*, Harry N. Abrams, New York 1959; Sam Hunter, *J. Miró, L'Œuvre gravé*, Calmann-Lévy, Paris 1958.

Edouard Goerg
Photo André Villers

EDOUARD GOERG

Born in Sydney (Australia) on June 9, 1893; died at Callian (France) on April 13, 1969. Lived in Australia and England up to the age of seven, when his family settled in Paris. Studied at the Collège Gerson and the Lycée Janson de Sailly. In 1912 entered the Académie Ranson, where Maurice Denis and Paul Sérusier were teachers. After the war, took up painting again. Exhibited his work in the Salons of 1922 and did his first prints in that year. In 1923 met Laboureur, who encouraged him to continue engraving. His first plates were drypoint engravings on zinc, but he soon gave that up for copper. Produced a steady flow of etchings, which he exhibited at the Salon de l'Araignée and the Peintres-Graveurs Indépendants, whose Founder and President was Laboureur. Many of his prints were published by H.-M. Petiet. His finest productions include *Men and Gods, The Birds Driven out of the Sky, The War of the Gods.* In 1944 Goerg took up lithography on Jacques Villon's advice, first in black and white and later in color. Did book illustration: *The Apocalypse* (twenty lithographs in black and white), *The Book of Job* (twenty etchings), *Les Fleurs du Mal* (three hundred lithographs in black and white), Dante's *Inferno* (fifty etchings). Goerg did some seven hundred and fifty prints, of which three hundred were as separate plates and four hundred and fifty as book illustrations.

Bibliography: Edouard Goerg, Crès, Paris 1929; Thieffry, *L'Œuvre gravé de Goerg,* Catalogue, Thesis Ecole du Louvre, typescript 1953; Bibl. Nat., *Œuvre gravé de Goerg*, Catalogue, Paris 1963; M. Avati, *Album des Peintres-Graveurs français, 80e Anniversaire*, Paris 1969.

ANDRÉ MASSON

Born at Balagny on January 4, 1896. Studied at the Académie des Beaux-Arts in Brussels. In 1912 went to Paris on Verhaeren's advice. In 1922 met Kahnweiler, who put him in a position to devote himself to painting. Underwent the influence of Cubism and Juan Gris. In 1923 painted *The Four Elements*, which attracted the attention of André Breton. In 1924 joined the Surrealists, did automatic gesture drawings and his first etchings for his first illustrated book, G. Limbour's *Soleil bas.* In 1925 did his first lithographs for Michel Leiris's first book, *Simulacre*. Masson has done a lot of book illustration, for example, *Toro* by Leiris and a splendid *Voyage à Venise* (1952) with forty-one color lithographs. He is passionately interested in engraving and has invented new techniques: insufflation, projection, tachism, action painting. Though he has not foresworn lithography—far from it—he feels that there is more scope for adventure in copperplate engraving because it introduces a powerful re-agent, the acid, which he employs diluted with only one-tenth of water. For Masson, "engraving is infinity." From 1941 to 1945 he stayed in the United States, where he did a quantity of lithographs in black and white, among them *Bestiary* and *The Genius of Ruins*, for which, like Delacroix, he used the scraper. Like Redon, he has a passion for transfer paper in which he sees a certain mystery to be investigated. After discovering the color lithographs of Bonnard and Vuillard, he found pleasure in working in that medium at Mourlot's. His graphic *œuvre* totals over five hundred prints, more than half of which are lithographs and two-thirds in color.

André Masson
Photo Louise Leiris

Bibliography: Das graphische Werk von A. Masson, Radierungen und Lithographien, 1954; A. Masson, *Entretiens avec G. Charbonnier*, 1958; Jean Hugues, *50 Ans d'Edition de D. H. Kahnweiler*, Galerie Louise Leiris, Paris 1959; M. Avati, *Album des Peintres-Graveurs français, 80e Anniversaire*, Paris 1969.

Salvador Dali
Photo Roger Viollet

SALVADOR DALI

Born at Figueras (Catalonia) on May 11, 1904. His father was a notary public from Dali's spiritual hometown, Cadaquès. Desultory schooling at Figueras, first drawing lessons. Academy of Fine Arts in Madrid. Devoured philosophical works and Freud. Discovered, in magazines, Cubism, Futurism and Metaphysical Art. Formed a close friendship with Federico Garcia Lorca. One-man shows in Barcelona in 1925 and in Madrid in 1926. Harmonized the example of Gris, de Chirico and Carrà with the refined methods of the Old Masters. Traveled by taxi to Paris to meet Picasso; visited Versailles and the Musée Grévin (waxworks). Discovered Surrealism. Married Gala Eluard. Developed "paranoiac-critical activity," a delirious system strongly influenced by psycho-analysis. In 1937 a journey to Italy led to a break with Surrealism and a reversion to the Renaissance. In 1940 Dali went to the United States. After the war he settled at Cadaquès. In his art he has succeeded in achieving the synthesis of what André Breton called a retrograde craft with the most extreme inventions of modern culture. His graphic *œuvre* comprises etchings and lithographs, which have evolved parallel to his paintings. Has illustrated Lautréamont's *Chants de Maldoror* (1934) with forty-two etchings, *The Divine Comedy* and *Don Quixote* with lithographs, and *Tristan et Iseut* with drypoints.

Bibliography: S. Dali, *La Vie secrète de S. Dali*, La Table ronde, Paris 1942; S. Dali, *Journal d'un Génie*, La Table ronde, Paris 1964; Tsunetaka Ueda, *S. Dali Exhibition*, Catalogue, Tokyo 1964.

Bernard Lorjou

BERNARD LORJOU

Born at Blois on September 9, 1908. Self-taught. Painted his parents' portraits when fourteen years old. At a very early age decided to be a painter and made a vain attempt to obtain admission to the Ecole des Arts Décoratifs in Paris. At fourteen he was alone in Paris, with no money but determined to paint. Finally found a job in the designing office of an important Lyons silk manufacturer, Francis Ducharne, in the Cité Tourlaque. There he met Yvonne Mottet, his lifelong companion, and completed his artistic and intellectual development from 1924 to 1930. Lorjou is a painter who bears witness and nothing human is foreign to him. His painting caught the eye of Fernand Mourlot, who let him use his workshop free of charge and initiated him in lithography in 1948. Lorjou has done over one hundred and fifty lithographs in black and white and in color, including *The Bourgeois of Paris, Fools* and *Flowers*. Through his friend Jacques Frélaut he learnt etching, a medium he has used to produce over one hundred plates in black and white and in color. At Robert Blanchet's he did the blocks for his *Bestiary*—thirty-eight woodcuts in two, three or four colors. In 1969 Jean Schneider commissioned one hundred copper-plate engravings on the bullfight and Sommer ordered fifty on the denizens of the forest for the Musée de la Chasse. In this work Lorjou obtained extraordinary effects by combining different techniques. The first plates for his *Tauromachy* have splendid force and drive.

Bibliography: J. P. Crespelle, *Montmartre vivant, Lorjou*, Chapter 10, Hachette, Paris 1964; Galerie A. Gattlen, *Catalogue*, Lausanne 1965.

Alfred Manessier
Photo Foto-Pitz A.R.P.S.,
Bocholt, Germany

ALFRED MANESSIER

Born at Saint-Ouen on December 5, 1911. Attended the Ecole des Beaux-Arts at Asnières and later in Paris. In 1929 copied the Old Masters in the Louvre. Attended the art schools in Montparnasse. Studied architecture at the Académie Ranson. In 1933 exhibited in the Salon des Indépendants. From 1936 to 1940 his paintings were still influenced by Surrealism. This influence was definitively eliminated by the war, leaving him with a more personal vision derived from Cubism and Fauvism and prompted by his conversion in

1943. In that year Manessier did his first line engraving, *L'Atelier du Bignon*. In 1944 a second line engraving of the studio with the painter at work displays a Piranesian architecture with magnificent light effects. In 1948, his first lithograph (in black and white). In 1949, seven lithographs on the theme of Easter. In 1958, *The Spiritual Canticles of St. John of the Cross* (twelve lithographs), followed by *The Dedication of Beauce to Our Lady of Chartres* (fifty lithographs). Manessier's graphic *œuvre* comprises five or six line engravings and some one hundred and thirty lithographs. So far he has not done any etchings, woodcuts or aquatints.

Bibliography: C. Bourniquel, *Trois Peintres: Le Moal, Manessier, Singier*, R. Drouin, Paris 1946; B. Dorival, "A. Manessier, Artisan religieux" in *L'Œil*, 10, Paris 1955.

Antoni Clavé

ANTONI CLAVÉ

Born in Barcelona on April 5, 1913. At thirteen attended night classes at the Barcelona Art School. At seventeen did drawings for magazines. Publicity posters. In 1935 these activities took up all his time and he virtually gave up painting. In 1939 he went to France. Showed his drawings and gouaches at Perpignan. Reached Paris in April of that year. First lithographs. Newspaper illustrations. In 1941 he settled in Montparnasse. Influenced by Bonnard and Vuillard and in 1944 by Picasso on their first meeting. Began to illustrate books with lithographs in black and white. In 1950 started work on his famous *Gargantua*, which led him to renovate his subject matter with the series of the *Big Playing-Card Kings*. Medieval figures. *Homage to Zurbaran*. In 1955 devoted himself to painting : series of *Bearded Kings*, *Queens*, and *Knights in Armor*. In 1956 awarded the Grand Prix for Engraving at the Venice Biennale (UNESCO). In 1957, Sao Paulo; in 1958, Tokyo. In 1964, member of the Society of French Painter-Engravers. In 1965 executed thirteen lithographs for his *Homage to Domenikos Theotokopoulos*. In 1966, his first etchings : three in black and white, the rest in color. In 1968 executed large color aquatints (plates measuring 70×50 cm). All in all Clavé's graphic *œuvre* comprises three hundred works, of which two hundred are lithographs in black and white or in color for book illustration and a hundred are separate prints, namely seventy lithographs and some thirty etchings and aquatints. Only one linocut.

Bibliography: Pierre Osenat, *Eloge d'Antoni Clavé* (with eight original lithographs), Manuel Bruker, Paris; Jean Cassou, *Antoni Clavé par Sala Gaspar*, Rauter, Barcelona 1960; Galerie Creuzevault, *A. Clavé, Tapisseries, Assemblages, Peintures, Gouaches, Œuvres 1962–1968*, Paris 1968; M. Avati, *Album des Peintres-Graveurs français, 80e Anniversaire*, Paris 1969.

MICHEL CIRY

Born at La Baule on August 31, 1919. Studied in Paris. Showed a precocious taste for linework, which led him to execute engravings at the age of sixteen. At nineteen was invited to the "Contemporary Artists' Exhibition" in the Petit Palais, where he showed for the first time a set of drawings and prints. In 1939 executed thirty-nine etchings and aquatints. In 1940, forty-one plates, including some drypoints and his first woodcut. Greatly admired were *The Flight into Egypt* and, still more, *Big Roofs in the Snow*. In 1941, on the initiative of Jacques Beltrand, was made a member of the Society of French Painter-Engravers. His prints were typical of a very young artist in possession of great technical skill and revealed a certain gravity of inspiration that interested Segonzac, Villon and Goerg. First lithographs and first book illustrations at this time. From 1942 to 1948 the medium he most frequently employed was the drypoint, which he used with astonishing delicacy. In 1949 his vision changed, as can be seen in the etching *Jesus*. Since then he has never reverted to his former manner but has continued to engrave faces with an intense human and divine expression. Ciry has illustrated a great many books, among them

Michel Ciry
Photo M. Bugnion-Rosset

Mario Avati

Dominique by Fromentin, *Madame Bovary* by Flaubert, *Farces Normandes* by Maupassant, *Le Voyageur sur la Terre* by Green, *L'Annonce faite à Marie* by Claudel and, most important of all, *Génitrix* by Mauriac. To date Ciry's graphic *œuvre* totals over a thousand prints.

Bibliography: Arthur W. Heintzelman, "Prints of Michel Ciry" in *The Boston Public Library Quarterly*, 1953; B. Champigneules, "Michel Ciry le Graveur-Peintre," in *Plaisir de France*, 1956; N. Cailler, "M. Ciry," in *Documents*, 70, Geneva 1957; F. Mauriac, "Michel Ciry" in *Jardin des Arts*, 131, Paris 1965; F. Daulte, *Michel Ciry*, La Bibliothèque des Arts, Paris 1966; R. Passeron, *L'Œuvre gravé, 1949–1954*, La Bibliothèque des Arts, Paris 1968; R. Passeron, *L'Œuvre gravé, 1955–1968*, La Bibliothèque des Arts, Paris 1969; R. Passeron, *Michel Ciry, L'Œuvre gravé, 1935–1948* (not yet published).

MARIO AVATI

Born at Monaco on May 27, 1921. In 1936 was admitted to the Ecole des Arts décoratifs in Nice. In 1940 left school and set to work alone, producing almost monochrome paintings of lawyers, judges and jesters besides a quantity of drawings. Decided to go to Paris and in 1947 was admitted to the Ecole des Beaux-Arts, where his chief interest was engraving. Worked with Robert Cami, who taught line engraving, but his first prints were exclusively etchings, drypoints and aquatints. Was passionately interested in drawing—in twenty years has done over eight thousand—and devoted himself intensely to engraving. In 1949 produced his first lithographs. Goerg discovered Avati in 1950 and gave him some good advice. The Salon d'Automne. Showed gouaches and colored drawings in New York; small engravings in Paris. First mezzotint. In 1951 engraved *Les Cyclopes* and *Les Extravagants*. Michel Ciry presented him to the Society of French Painter-Engravers. In 1952–3, *Les Ridicules* followed by etchings, woodcuts and linocuts. In 1957, the first of the large mezzotints that have been his major interest for the last twelve years. Avati has illustrated *A l'Aube d'une Guerre* by Ph. de Rothschild, *Chiméra* by Lewis Carroll, *Les Contes Cruels* by Villiers de l'Isle-Adam, *La Médecine Arabe* by R. Arnaldez and *Aphorismes, Menus et Variétés* by Brillat-Savarin—over five hundred prints in all.

Bibliography: Irving Haas, "The Print Collector" in *Art News*, 1951; Fatou, *Mario Avati*, Fontaine, La Féria 1953; J.-R. Thome, "Avati, Etude sur ses Livres illustrés" in *Le Courrier graphique*, Paris 1957; P. Cailler, "Avati" in *Documents*, 96, Geneva 1958; G. A. Dassonville, *Les Livres illustrés par Avati*, Le Brûlot, Paris 1964; E.-H. Bloch, *Avati, Prints from 1957 to 1967*, Grunwald Graphic Art Foundation, Los Angeles 1967; R. Hirsch, *En Manière noire: Prints by Mario Avati*, Allentown Art Museum 1968; Roger Passeron, *L'Œuvre gravé de Mario Avati*, Vol. 1, Bibliothèque des Arts, Paris (not yet published).

LARS BO

Born at Koldnig (Denmark) on May 29, 1924. 1940–2, studied at the Copenhagen Academy of Applied Art. In 1947 went to Paris and settled in Montparnasse. Studied engraving. Illustrated books and contributed drawings to international reviews. Since 1958 has devoted all his time to engraving and watercolor painting. In 1959 awarded First Prize for Engraving at the Paris Biennale. Has executed magnificent color aquatints, some of them heightened with point and burin. His book illustrations include *Chambres d'Inquiétude* (1959); *Cris de Paris* (1960); Gogol's *Le Manteau* (1961); *Le Meneur d'Ombres* (1962), one of his handsomest books; *La Main Enchantée* by Gérard de Nerval (1965); the delightful *Reine des Neiges* after a fairytale by Hans Christian Andersen (1968); *Le Lac des Cygnes* (1969). At present Lars Bo is intensely interested in engraving on lithographic stone, which he works up with burin and point, as in *La Plume retrouvée*. So far he has produced some two hundred and fifty prints; they include five color lithographs but the majority are color aquatints. He has not yet done any woodcuts.

Lars Bo

Bibliography: F. Madsen and R. Giraud, *L'Œuvre gravé de Lars Bo*, Catalogue Galerie Carit Andersen, Copenhagen 1965; R. Barotte, "Lars Bo" in *Plaisir de France*, Paris December 1968; M. Avati, *Album des Peintres-Graveurs français, 80ᵉ Anniversaire*, Paris 1969.

Jacques Ramondot
Photo Vasari

JACQUES RAMONDOT

Born in Paris on May 21, 1928. After high-school, attended the Ecole Nationale des Beaux-Arts in Paris from 1947 to 1953. His teachers were Galanis, Cami and Goerg. While at art school he took up engraving, producing one hundred and fifty plates that have not been preserved. In 1954 won the first Grand Prix de Rome for copperplate engraving and was a boarder at the Villa Medici till 1958. In 1959 appointed professor of drawing and engraving at the Ecole des Beaux-Arts in Rouen, a post he still holds. 1963, Prix Félix Fénéon. Ramondot is a member of the committee of the Society of French Painter-Engravers and of the National Committee for Engraving and Book Illustration. He has never touched lithography, except for two or three invitations or announcements. His *œuvre* totals some two hundred and eighty prints, of which one hundred and twenty for book illustration—fifty etchings for Guillaume Apollinaire's *L'Hérésiarque et Cie* (1959); twenty drypoints for Théophile Gautier's *Venise* (1962); twenty-five etchings for Blaise Cendrars's *Du Monde entier* (1967) and twenty-seven etchings for *L'Or* by the same author (1969).

Bibliography: W. J. Strachan, "Contemporary French Beaux Livres" in *The Connoisseur*, London Sept. 1964; J. Frapier, *Galerie des Peintres-Graveurs, Cat. V*, Paris 1968; M. Avati, *Album des Peintres-Graveurs français, 80ᵉ Anniversaire*, Paris 1969.

BERNARD BUFFET

Born in Paris on July 10, 1928. A child of Paris, his early years were spent, sad and solitary, on the Rue des Batignoles. At the age of fifteen he attended night school and started to do charcoal drawings. In 1944 was admitted to the Ecole des Beaux-Arts in Paris but only stayed a few months because the teaching disgusted him. Preferred to study the works of David, Rembrandt, and particularly Courbet in the Louvre. Discovered Permeke, Ensor, and more especially Gruber. In 1946 exhibited in the Salon of the Under-Thirties. At nineteen was admitted to the Salon des Indépendants and the Salon d'Automne. In 1948 a collector named Girardin made a scene because Buffet was rejected by the jury of the Exhibition of Young Painting. His first engraving, a drypoint, dates from 1948; his second from 1949; his third from 1950—two self-portraits and a likeness of Jean Giono. Since then he has done one hundred and twenty-five drypoints for *Les Chants de Maldoror*. Has also illustrated Giono's *Recherche de la Pureté*, Cocteau's *La Voix humaine* and *St. Cast, Souvenir d'Enfance*. Took up lithography in 1952. His first three lithographs were commissioned by P. Cailler's Guilde de la Gravure; the next two for Jacometti's *Œuvre Gravé*. So far he has done some three hundred and eighty prints, including three hundred drypoints, five lithographs in black and white and seventy-five lithographs in color.

Bernard Buffet
Photo Galerie M. Garnier

Bibliography: P. Descargues, *Bernard Buffet*, Paris 1950; J.-R. Thome, "Bernard Buffet" in *Courrier graphique*, pp. 3–10, Sept. Oct. 1955; F. Mourlot, *Bernard Buffet, Œuvre gravé: Lithographies 1952–1966*, Mazo, Paris 1967; G. F. Reinz, *Bernard Buffet–Gravures, Engravings, Radierungen, 1948–1967*, Orangerie, Cologne 1968; M. Avati, *Album des Peintres-Graveurs français, 80ᵉ Anniversaire*, Paris 1969.

The text, the illustrations in four colour offset, and the jacket of this book were printed by Imprimerie Paul Attinger S.A., Neuchâtel, and the black-and-white illustrations by Roto-Sadag S.A., Geneva. – The photolitho work for the four colour illustrations was executed by Busag S.A., Berne, and for the black-and-white illustrations by Atesa, Geneva. – The binding was entrusted to Karl Hanke, Düsseldorf. – The lay-out is the work of André Rosselet, Auvernier.

Printed in Switzerland